SILENT BANK HEIST IN TEXAS

THERE IS A BLACK-OWNED BANK HIDDEN INSIDE OTHER BANKS …

MARILYN OLIVER

Published by:
RH Publishing
Dallas, Texas
www.rhpublishingcompany.com

ISBN# 978-1-960494-31-3

Some of the names have been changed for individual privacy.

Front cover: Photo was taken in 1917. The men pictured were considered to be the bank officers at that time.

Book cover design, photos, and editing by Marilyn Oliver.

DEDICATION

Mr. Keith Milberger
1949-2017

This book is dedicated to Keith Milberger. He was a very kind, considerate, and generous gentleman. Keith genuinely loved helping people. His compassion for life was contagious for those fortunate enough to spend time with him. I was especially blessed by God for allowing Mr. Milberger to cross paths with me!

ACKNOWLEDGMENTS

I want to thank my parents, Robert Oliver, Jr. and Henrietta Oliver, for their support and for traveling with me while I was researching the Farmers and Citizens Savings Bank.

I want to thank my sister, Mardella Marsh, for her support.

I want to thank my children, Patricia Oliver, Charlotte Pittman, Tammy James, and William Gardner, Sr., for understanding why it was so important for me to put in the time and the years it has taken to do the research.

I want to thank my grandchildren, Jazelle Gardner, Jayden Gardner, Jalaya Gardner, Jordin Gardner, Jonet Gardner, William Gardner, Jr., and La Fion Pennington, for all the love that they have given me when I would share the great memories I had experienced when I came to the end and needed their encouragement.

I want to thank my friends and associates for assisting me in doing the research. Leila Hallan, Liz Bennett, Regionald Browne, Versalean Logans, Karen Ross, Mary Sharpee, Tim Lynch, Maria Rojo, Rowin White, Gracelynn White, Janet Anderson, Steve Jones (Cowboy), Vette Jones, Doris Jackson, Shirley Hampton, Sarah Anderson, Patricia Rogers,

Albert Charles Brewer, Jr., Isiko Muhammad, Dr. Leicha Shaver, Pastor Joseph Mwenya, Lilian and Johnny Aldama, Kay and Scott McVittie, Ferrell and Nick Fellows, Jennifer Davis, and Carla Bryan.

FOREWORD

"A BANK HEIST COMMITTED IN PLAIN SIGHT"

In 1926, a heinous crime was committed—a bank heist—and it was committed in plain sight! Now this was not an unusual crime to occur during this era. However, the story that would ensure this crime would come to light is now almost 100 years later. The amazing part is the way that it has surfaced is far more interesting than the actual Bank Heist event itself.

So, how or who has brought this crime to light? Marilyn Oliver is her name. She may not be known to many people now, but mark my words, once you have read this book and watched the movie, that is in the making, you will not forget this 5' 2" woman.

I am Dr. Leicha Shaver, an educational leader, who is currently serving as CEO and founder of Advanced Preparatory International (API), as well as the Co-Founder and President of Texas Seminary Christian University in Dallas, Texas. My educational career spans more than 30 years, beginning in Tulsa as a teacher, college professor, and acquiring my assignment as a principal. This role would lead to transformative administrative roles in Dallas, Texas. Each experience led me closer to the day I would meet Marilyn Oliver at Advanced Preparatory International.

There is no question my meeting Marilyn was a chance encounter; it was ordained by a higher power than any of us. Her grandson was enrolled into API, and we met as a result. The meeting would lead to her grand-daughters attending, other family members, her neighbor's children and a host of other young men in particular, who she was able to convince, to complete High School.

As a result of meeting Marilyn, dozens of lives have been changed for the better. It is because of her tenacity that I believe God chose her for this very mission. She is not a woman that can be dismissed, discouraged, or duped. She may be small in stature, but she is definitely strong and mighty in the Lord. I have watched her persist for years to bring this amazing and powerful project to life.

This book will definitely impact many lives.

Dr. Leicha Shaver
CEO/Founder Advanced Preparatory International (API)
Co-Founder/President Texas Seminary Christian University
Dallas, Texas

TABLE OF CONTENTS

INTRODUCTION

As a child, I had many dreams, but there was one dream in particular that kept returning. Even as I grew older, this one dream with just a couple of variations, kept appearing.

The dream was this … I was always in this room, staring at this one corner. And in the corner, it was always a mess … with dirt or other trash just piled up in the corner.

I'm not sure why it took me so long, but I finally decided to ask the Lord,

"What does this mean?"

It was only then that the Lord began to lead me on this journey. A journey that has lasted 40 years in trying to resolve the bottomline issue that caused me to see this dirty mess that had been hidden, shoved in the corner, so no one would have access to it.

Keep in mind, as you continue to read this story, that what is revealed and I have written about has been passed down through several generations. The man who first told what happened, my great-grandfather, Allison Gardner, Sr., was very much alive and was a huge participant/victim in the criminal act that took place against him and other Blacks who lived in Palestine, Texas, at that time.

However, because of his race, he could only gain the facts or information from rumors that had spread around the town and community where he lived. As you read what was told to him, you will see the truth and the reason it has been hidden for so long—and by so many—and how others, when over the years were asked to help, they refused to even try to aid in resolving the problem because of the overwhelming outcome.

For most, fear itself has kept those who would have the knowledge and the ability to help to back down because of the devasting, illegal outcome that has already affected so many.

For me, I have had to learn to trust God in working hard to discover the facts to bring this horrible, illegal act to light. The Word states pretty clearly whatever is done in darkness will be brought to the light.

> "For nothing is secret, that shall not be made manifest;
> neither anything hid, that shall not be known
> and come abroad" (Luke 8:17, KJV).

It's time for the light to shine!
Let me share my journey with you.

Chapter 1

FROM PRINCESS TO GREEN PEACHES

On a hotter than hot summer day in July, I decided to visit my "Aunt Bertha," who once lived in Palestine, Texas. Palestine is about 100 miles south of Dallas. At the time, Aunt Bertha, who had been nicknamed "Birdie," was an elderly woman, well-educated and refined. As I drove up to her house, I noticed she was outside in the Texas heat picking peaches from her peach tree.

I drove over to where she was, rolled down my window and shouted, "Aunt Birdie, why are you out here in this heat?"

Now, Aunt Birdie was always excited to see me when I came to visit her. I exited the car and gave her a big hug and kiss. "Let me help you," I said, as I took the sack of green peaches from her. I slipped my arm under her arm for support, and we began to walk toward the house.

After talking and catching up some, I saw that it was getting to be about dinner time, so I asked her, "What's for dinner?" She shrugged her shoulders and stated she wasn't very hungry. She was just going to have a few of those green peaches and watch a little TV.

I truly thought Aunt Birdie was kidding. So, I walked toward the kitchen to see what I could find to prepare for us to eat dinner. I went through the cabinets and the refrigerator. I noticed there was nothing, absolutely nothing in the house to eat. There was only ice in the ice trays and those little green peaches were everywhere.

Puzzled and confused, I asked her, "Where is your food?" She pretended not to hear me and just kept watching TV. I asked again … she slowly turned to me and said, "I will go to the store next week once my check comes in." (Aunt Birdie was a retired school teacher who lived off of her small monthly pension.) Without hesitation I said, "Let's go and get you some food in this house and in your belly."

She agreed, so we got in the car and went to the grocery store. Once we returned, we began to put the groceries away. She then stated she had something important she needed to tell me. She disappeared into the back room of the house, and after several minutes, she emerged with an old silver box that had an elaborate engraving on it. She placed the box on the kitchen table and asked me to have a seat. She said she had something to share with me. Something she said I must know about—her, her family, and the town of Palestine, Texas.

She began by telling me about her Grandpa Green. Aunt Birdie gazed softly. She said, "Daddy said the land would always carry our stories." She explained how Grandpa Green had built churches. He had a strong belief in faith and the community. He taught us to make the most out of life, and it all began in Palestine, Texas.

She continued with Grandpa Green's life was one that emphasized resilience, determination, and leadership, during one of the most challenging eras in American history. Working as a slave, on the Elias Oldham Plantation in Texas, his early years were marked as having relentless labor and systematic oppression. Despite these hardships, he immersed as a symbol of progress, leaving a lasting legacy for both his family and the community.

Grandpa was the eldest child and his family was forced to move to Texas. They had endured the brutality of slavery, but they remained united. The Oldham Plantation became the Butler Plantation, and when C.L. Butler passed away in 1917, Mrs. Butler, his wife, wanted nothing to do with it, so she sold it to my dad, Allison, for $300.00. After the Emancipation in 1865, both Grandpa and daddy chose to remain on the Butler Plantation as free men, leveraging their knowledge of the land and their relationship with the Butlers to secure resources that were otherwise acceptable to freedom.

She went on to say that her Grandpa had understood that land was a valuable path to stability and generational progress. His entrepreneurial spirit was matched by his dedication to community upliftment. He worked with a minister there to help establish four key churches. These churches served as spiritual sanctuaries and hubs for education, community organization, and economic empowerment.

Grandpa also understood the importance of education. Despite the social challenges at the time, he made sure my dad learned to read and write, so he could be equipped to live in a prejudiced society.

She paused for a moment and took a deep breath. I could tell this wasn't going to be easy for her. At 88 years of age, the memories coming from this box were a lot for her to manage. Slowly she began to open the box, which was filled with old pictures and documents. The first picture she took out was of her father, Allison Gardner. Even though he had grown up as the son of slaves, he had a bigger than life character.

He had become a millionaire by the age of 22, in 1894. This was unheard of in the U.S., and even more unbelievable in the south. She began to share how her dad had owned a very large cotton gin and around 1,000 acres of land. This land had been part of the Butler estate, which he and his father had been loaned in exchange for their pay. In the early 1920s, he was considered the most powerful and successful Negro in Anderson County and was respected by both whites and Blacks.

Aunt Birdie continued to explain that there was something almost magical about her father, as if he had a gift to help restore and make things whole after the devastating horrors of slavery ... it was as if he was there to lead the way. With the land he owned, he no longer did a lot of manual labor. He had sharecroppers who worked for him. His job was to supervise and oversee the farm, checking on the sharecroppers, and … acting like he had seen the rich, white men do that they had all worked for at one time.

"Daddy was the first black man to own a car in Palestine," Birdie continued. "Truthfully, he had so much money that he could just about buy whatever he wanted whenever he wanted. It was the local custom for Black people to have to wait until Saturday to go into town. However, Daddy would make trips into town on any day of the week."

She then continued, "I never wanted for anything when I was growing up. I always had the finest of everything, the best education, etc." She had this lifestyle because of being a central part of an aristocratic, emerging class of Black Americans, and the socialites from around the country. She continued to talk about how she and her friends would travel the country for days and months, vacationing and visiting family and friends, regardless of where they lived.

When she completed her teacher's certification and landed her first teaching job, her father built her a beautiful home and furnished it with the finest furniture, carpet, and rugs he could find. As she explained it, her father's burden was to restore the Black family and their community.

"At that time, there was a strong movement taking place, not only in Texas, but nationally to make the Black man, his family, and his community whole through education and economic independence. My father, like many others, believed this was the only way Blacks could be truly free in America," she explained.

Aunt Birdie went on to say that her father had told her to not forget Jimmy's kids before she died. Jimmy was one of the many children her dad had fathered. After she had her second heart attack, she knew she needed to reach out to Jimmy, but since he had already passed, she reached out to his children. She discovered that his two younger children were in the restaurant business. Aunt Birdie was so pleased to find them and to be able to talk with them again.

Then she continued to tell me more of the story about what had happened, and the part I needed to play in it.

Farmers and Citizens Savings Bank Officers in 1917

Chapter 2

THE BANK IN PALESTINE, TEXAS

Aunt Birdie fixed herself a cup of tea and began to tell me more of the story. In 1906, her father, Allison, along with eight other prominent Black leaders from the community, started the first African American bank in Palestine, Texas. They called it Farmers and Citizen's Savings bank. She went on to describe the Bank as not just a financial institution. It actually was a living testimony to the African American experience because it emerged at a time when Blacks faced discrimination and had limited access to financial institutions. It was also during a season when Blacks were being freed from slavery.

This bank was recognized nationally by such leaders as Booker T. Washington, an American educator, author, and orator, who was the primary leader in the African American community, and Maggie Walker, the self-made millionaire and hair-care-magnate from Virginia. The bank supported many Black farmers, businesses, schools, and doctors. The bank was the lifeblood for Black independence in Palestine.

Birdie began to add how some of the other places in Palestine originated. James B. McKnight had moved to Anderson

County in 1848. In 1876, he bought land at this site and named it the McKnight Plaza. McKnight died in 1907, and in 1910, the Farmers and Citizens Savings Bank purchased the Plaza, which then became known as the "Square." It would become the center of Black commerce and culture. It was the main gathering place for Blacks in Palestine, Texas, for many years.

In the "Square" you could find all types of merchants selling goods and services, from doctors, dentists, a drug store, a cafe, a restaurant, a cab company, an accounting office, an insurance company, a barber shop, a dry cleaners, a theater, an entertainment hall, and even a funeral home.

Aunt Birdie stated she was a little girl when all this was going on, but she remembered it well. She also remembered that everywhere she went with her father, people wanted to speak to him or shake his hand. They would refer to him as the "King of Palestine" and I was the "Princess of Palestine." She smiled as she went on to say, “This name has actually stayed with me throughout my entire life.”

Aunt Birdie continued her story by claiming, “Life was great in Palestine, Texas, for many Blacks,” and it was mainly because the Bank provided a way for them to not only have financial security, but economic independence, which allowed many to thrive, to be able to afford to send their children to schools and colleges, to build homes, and to start businesses.

However, her voice changed as she said, “We would often read reports or hear rumors about how whites in the nearby counties were threatening the Black independent cities and communities.”

She continued with telling about this time in history. The trend of attacking independent Black communities and destroying and taking their property by angry whites was growing throughout the South, from Florida to Oklahoma, and even in parts of the North. So as we enjoyed the prosperity of our communities, we were well aware of the threat it posed to an angry white community.

This eventually became more than a rumor when Blacks were massacred in the city of Slocum by angry whites who were jealous of their prosperity. Slocum was a city located in Anderson County, which was less than ten miles south of Palestine.

"The Slocum massacre not only killed the people, but it destroyed a very prosperous, independent Black community. It was a sad day for sure."

She paused and took a long breath … and then decided to totally change the subject. "After I finished college, my parents let me travel the country during the summer with my friends. We traveled as far as Los Angeles, St. Louis, Chicago and New York for sometimes months at a time. In 1923, while visiting my brothers in Chicago, I met the love of my life, Dr. Luther Johnson, a prominent African American doctor. We married, and I moved to Chicago to join him."

With the biggest smile on her face, she stated, "Living in Chicago and being married to Dr. Johnson turned out to be the best time of my life."

However, during the following years, things began to fall apart back home in Palestine, Texas.

Chapter 3

ROYALL NATIONAL BANK'S "TAKE OVER" PLAN

It was time for Royall National Bank to hold their quarterly board meeting where the CFO, Mr. Smith, presented the bank's profit and loss statement. The news was worse than the previous four quarterly reports. And this quarter they had recorded their sixth foreclosure—the latest casualty—the Davis farm. So far, within a 12-month period, they had already experienced a total of 17 foreclosures.

CFO Mr. Smith slowly raised his head, his eyes piercing over the glasses that were perched on his nose. The tension was great, especially for him, because he was going to have to tell the members of the board that the bank was heading toward bankruptcy. Literally, it was not going to be able to pay its depositors, and in fact, if there was a run on the bank that day, they would not be able to pay their depositors what they owed them.

He said, "We have about four months to come up with the funds that have been lost due to the bank's bad investments." The room became uncomfortably silent. Royall National Bank had been a pillar in the community for decades. Now, for them to go bankrupt and possibly close—it would destroy the city of Palestine and Anderson County, since most of its citizens had deposits and their entire life's savings in this bank.

The Board Members began to throw out ideas. Board member, Commissioner Mr. Wilson, leaned forward, with his face turning bright red, he began to lay out an apocalyptic scene—which would be the result if Royall could not pay its depositors. He continued by explaining how the new rail system would have to lay off hundreds of workers, which would mean that families would not be able to buy food or pay their bills. He stressed that the town's people would not be ready for this kind of crisis.

His tone changed. "Worse yet," he interjected, "the Nigger bank" will be the only sovereign financial institution for miles. This would end up forcing the white people to depend on Niggers for their survival.

After discussing any options at length about the dire consequences of the bank closing down, the board agreed that closing was not and would never be an option. So, they began to discuss how they could come up with the money. At that time, the bank needed $1.3 million dollars to stay sovereign and to get through this crisis.

As the members continued to discuss their options, they soon realized that none of these ideas might even come close to creating the amount of money they needed to keep the bank open.

Board member, Mr. Charlie King, then stated he thought there might be a way for Royall National Bank to acquire the money it needed. He went on to state that many of the county's smaller banks were experiencing the same things that Royall was currently experiencing. The idea was maybe they should approach them to discuss a plan of merging together. He went on to say, "I know most of these boys, and if we present them with a good deal, they will take it." The board thought that sounded like a good idea, so they voted and unanimously agreed to implement Mr. King's plan.

For the first two months, everything seemed to be working in their favor. Royall National Bank merged with five smaller banks in the neighboring cities and counties. The deficit began to get quite a bit smaller. They thought things were going to work out.

However, the board met again to discuss if their plan to merge with the smaller banks was working. CFO Mr. Smith spoke up and began to update the board on the bank's progress in being able to find the funds to replace the $1.3 million dollar deficit. He informed the board that he had both good and bad news. "The good news," he began, "is that all of the smaller banks have agreed to consolidate. The bad news is that these banks are so small that the most we have been able to raise is $500,000. Obviously, this still falls short of the $1.3 million we need to stay sovereign."

There was a brief silence. Then Commissioner Mr. Wilson asked Mr. Smith if he had included Farmers and Citizens Savings Bank as one of the smaller banks to be consolidated. "The reason I'm asking," Mr. Wilson went on to say is, "I've heard they have over $90,000 cash on hand, and they also have over 1,000 prime acres of land. Together that should be worth at least one million dollars."

Mr. Smith looked at Mr. Wilson and laughed!!! "You know that's the Nigger's bank, right? We don't serve Niggers in our banks."

At that moment, board member, Mr. Jackson, who rarely spoke in these meetings, suddenly said, "There is a way to acquire the Nigger's bank's assets legally, and there is nothing they can do about it." He now had everyone's attention. He went on to explain, "It will require a little money from the bank to give us a proper standing in court, but I am sure my friend, Judge Dent, will see things our way. If we make a deposit in their bank and declare it a loan, we can then go before Judge Dent and declare our concerns that they are mismanaging their funds, and they cannot pay their depositors and creditors."

CFO Mr. Smith stated the idea was preposterous, and the Niggers would not allow such a thing to happen. Mr. Wilson then asked Mr. Smith, "Have you ever heard of the Texas Black Codes?"

Mr. Smith said, "Yes ... but what does that have to do with anything?"

Mr. Jackson then spoke up and replied, "According to the Texas Black Codes, Niggers can't contest a white man's word in any matter in a court of law. Therefore, Judge Dent will rule in our favor, and we will place Mr. Grigsby in receivership of the bank's assets, which he will deposit into Royall National Bank. This will solve our problems, gentlemen," he boasted.

Board member Mr. Brown protested. "This is completely immoral," he said, "and I want nothing to do with it."

Mr. Jackson then reminded the men that they only had 30 days left to keep the bank doors open and the crisis now would be even worse because they had consolidated five other banks into their bank. Now, their depositors would also suffer. But the very worst part on top of all of that would be the Niggers bank would be ruling Palestine, which in effect would make the white man a second-class-citizen.

Naturally, this was not the news they had hoped to hear. But they knew something was needing to be done and it had to be done immediately. Although no confirmed decision was made right then, later that evening, Mr. Jackson paid Judge Dent a visit at his house. Mr. Jackson explained to the judge what was taking place with Royall National Bank. He went on to explain that if it fails, the Nigger bank would be the only bank serving Palestine. With a Nigger bank the only bank in Palestine, it would make the white man a second-class-citizen to the Niggers.

Judge Dent asked, "What do you plan on doing?"

Mr. Jackson explained the desired solution to bring charges against the Farmers and Citizens Savings Bank for mismanagement and to implement the Texas Black Code. However, they were going to need the judges approval. Judge Dent agreed to go along with the scheme to seize Farmers and Citizens Savings Bank's assets.

The following day, Mr. Grigsby, the bank's CEO, was told to take a rare trip and visit with Farmers and Citizens Savings Bank. The reason Mr. Grigsby was selected to go to the bank was not only because of his current position but because he had been a runner for Royall National Bank since he was 12 years old. He had reported everything he had heard from day one about Farmers and Citizen's Savings Bank to the officials at Royall National Bank because all banks are required to have a corresponding bank and Royall National Bank was Farmers and Citizens Savings Bank's corresponding bank. So, the people at Farmers and Citizens Savings Bank also knew him.

The instructions Mr. Grigsby was told to follow was to express how he had heard that the Farmers and Citizens Savings Bank was really doing well, and they wanted to be a part of it by making a small loan to the bank at a below market interest rate. With skepticism Vice-Chairman, H.L. Price, accepted the $5,000 loan. It was only because Mr. Grigsby was well respected in the Black community that Mr. Price felt honored that Royall National Bank wanted to partner with them. This is the main reason he was willing to accept their loan offer.

Royall National Bank's "Take Over" Plan had started. It wouldn't be long now, and they would be filing a lawsuit against them.

BLACK CODES OF 1865

- THE BLACK CODES WERE INSTITUTED BY SOUTHERN LEGISLATIVE BODIES IN 1865 AND 1866 IN RESPONSE TO THE EMANCIPATION OF THE FOUR MILLION FORMER SLAVES IN THE SOUTHERN STATES DURING AND AFTER THE AMERICAN CIVIL WAR (1861-1865). THE BLACK CODES RECOGNIZED THE NEW STATUS OF AFRICAN AMERICANS AS FREED PEOPLE AND OFFERED THEM SOME OF THE BASIC RIGHTS OF CITIZENSHIP. HOWEVER, THE CODES ALSO DEFINED THE FREED PEOPLE AS LEGALLY SUBORDINATE TO WHITES AND ATTEMPTED TO MANAGE THEIR LABOR IN A WAY THAT WOULD CAUSE MINIMAL DISRUPTION TO THE LABOR SYSTEM INSTITUTED UNDER SLAVERY.

Chapter 4

SCHEME #2

At that time, Texas was experiencing one of its worst droughts in decades, and there was a dramatic reduction in cotton prices worldwide. Royall National Bank had invested heavily into these cotton farms, basing their decisions on the past war demands for cotton worldwide. However, now because of the falling prices of cotton, farmers were now dealing with the worst economic climate they had seen for decades. And as a result, they couldn't make their loan payments, causing the bank to foreclose on them.

So, the bank's deficit was not improving. Their dilemma was still up for a permanent solution that needed to happen immediately.

The Board met again. As if Scheme #1 wasn't bad enough, the unfair saga continued. Again, keep in mind, the reports of what was taking place in these board meetings was rumored all around the community, by both whites and Blacks. But because those who were cheated were Black, they were never ever allowed to be visible or participate in any of the official meetings in person.

After WWI, the U.S. Government had been training surveyors to use new technology and techniques to increase the accuracy for new oil discoveries. This new technology led to an oil explosion, and this discovery opened the first of the series of new oil fields in Texas and Oklahoma. These two states became the nation's top producers. The oil speculators were reporting that one of Texas' largest oil discoveries was in East Texas, in Anderson County, which included Palestine, Texas.

The annual Oil Prospectus Almanac, the holy grail for oil prospectors, was projecting that the next big oil discoveries would be made in Anderson County. The Mayor and the other city officials were excited to hear the news. They had invited the surveyors and oil companies to Palestine for the big announcement, and they were going to be there this week. They wanted them to present their findings, thus revealing what land and property the oil was on. Some of these spectators were projecting millions, even billions of barrels of oil were beneath the ground in Palestine, Texas.

This was not just important to them and their community, but to the U.S. at large because there had been an oil shortage. So, the executives came, and everyone in Palestine who owned property was invited to be at the big announcement, except for the Black land owners. The whole city was ablaze, hoping that their property would be identified as the land with the oil and minerals beneath it. The surveyors began to call out the coordinates of property they believed had oil beneath it, starting with the smallest reserves and moving on to the largest.

As they began to call out the coordinates, you would hear shouts of joyful celebration coming from the crowd as families discovered they had oil on their property and were going to be rich. At the conclusion of the announcement, the survey and oil company executive approached the city leaders to inform them that out of the 9,000 acres with oil reserves there was still 1,000 acres that remained unclaimed—and three of the largest oil reserves were underneath those 1,000 acres.

The city officials and surveyors rushed over to the County Clerk's office to identify who the owners of the 1,000 acres were. As they identified the property coordinates, they quickly realized the property was located in the Nigger sections of Palestine, and the property was owned by its' Black citizens.

As the County Clerk was about to announce the name of the 1,000 acres, the Mayor interrupted him. He then stated that he personally would inform everyone and deliver the good news to these property owners, who may not wish to be made known publicly. Of course, they realized who the true owners of this property belonged to—the Blacks. The surveyors and oil executives, not knowing who the property belonged to, stated whoever owns these lots will be the richest families in all of East Texas. The Mayor and the County Commissioner looked both shocked and bewildered. They stated that they would personally inform the owners of their new found fortunes.

As the city was celebrating its new wealth, there was food, music, and dancing flowing through the streets. The Mayor and the County Commissioner convened an emergency meeting with the other top officials and leaders—a group of seven men in the city and the county's most influential leaders—including Railroad Commissioner Mr. Taylor, Royall National Bank CEO Mr. Grigsby, County District Judge Dent, Sheriff Redder, and Mr. Malloy. These were the wealthiest men in Anderson County. They all gathered in their private place in the backroom of Tom's bar.

As the men came in one by one, each was bewildered as to why anyone would call a meeting in the middle of a festive day like today. As the men sat in the circle … Mayor Anderson, who was standing in the middle of the circle, began to tell the men why he and the County Commissioner called such an urgent meeting.

He began, "All you gentlemen are aware that the surveyors and oil companies were in town today to announce the big oil findings in Anderson County. Out of the 9,000 acres identified, there are 1,000 acres that are owned by Black families in Palestine, and according to the surveyors, this 1,000 acres contains three of the largest oil reserves that have ever been discovered in East Texas. These oil wells would make the owners of that property the richest families in East Texas.

"According to county records, 10 families own these 1,000 acres, and the largest owner is that Nigger, Allison Gardner, who already has more money than half the whites in Anderson County combined. Some even state that he is already a millionaire."

He continued, "According to the surveyors and oil executives, these families will be worth tens of millions of dollars. So what does this mean to Anderson County? It will mean that our venture way of life is about to change. Anderson County may be able to accept one or two wealthy Nigger families, but to have literally hundreds of wealthy Niggers in the city of Palestine … that will relegate the white man and his families as second-class-citizens or worse—servants to wealthy Niggers. We must do something to prevent this from happening," the Mayor exclaimed.

"What are our options?" asked the Railroad Commissioner.

"That's why we are here. We need to discuss our options," replied the Mayor.

"Do they know that their property has oil on it, Mayor?"

"No, they were not invited to the announcement today, and the official letters from the city, nor the oil company's notifications have been sent out to the property owners identifying their properties as the ones with the oil. According to our records, most of the Nigger farmers who own land are using it as collateral with the Nigger bank—the Farmers and Citizens Savings Bank. The other acres are privately owned by Nigger Gardner and his family.

"So, the way I see it, here are our options gentlemen … we can sit and let our great city be taken over by oil-rich Niggers, or we can purchase their property at today's value before they realize the value of the oil that is beneath it."

The men began to discuss the matter among themselves.

"They will never sell their land to a white man … not after today … the word will get around that there is oil in their fields," said Sheriff Redder.

The Mayor said, "We can order the oil company not to drill on Black-owned property without getting the approval from my office."

Judge Dent stood up and stated, "Those options are fine, but that will never work in the long run for Palestine's white citizens, if the property and oil stays in the hands of the Niggers. Some oil companies will eventually pay them to get the oil, making them and their children wealthier than the whites in Anderson County."

The Judge went on to say, "If the majority of the land is used for collateral and is held by Farmers and Citizens Savings Bank, then we must focus on ceasing the bank's assets. If we do this, we can ensure that that land and oil never falls into the hands of those Niggers. The remaining land belongs to Gardner and his family, they are already wealthy, and we can handle one wealthy Nigger family in Palestine."

Mayor Anderson was surprised by the Judge's remarks and stated, "Judge, if we cease Farmers and Citizens Savings Bank's assets for no reason, it will create a race riot in Anderson County. That will cause Federal troops to come to officiate."

The Judge then asked the Mayor, "Have you ever heard of the 'Texas Black Code?'"

The Mayor replied, "Yes, but it was outlawed seven years ago by the Federal Government."

"Yes, it was outlawed," said the Judge, "but the state of Texas, still enforces the spirit of the law."

"So, what does this mean, Judge?" asked the Mayor.

"It means if a white man stands in a Court of law against a Nigger, the Nigger cannot dispute or challenge that white man's word," said the Judge. What these men did not know was that the Judge had already been approached and was being paid to present this as an option by one of Royall's board members.

"So, explain to us how this works," said the Mayor.

The Judge began to explain how this would solve both of their issues—the lack of money in their $1.3 million debt and the land the oil is on. He started by saying, "If a white man has made a deposit in the Farmers and Citizens Savings Bank and then thinks the bank is doing things that are jeopardizing his deposits, or they are mismanaging, etc., he can come before the court and make a case to have the assets of the bank placed in receivership to secure his assets and the assets of the other depositors."

"Ok, so what do we have to do to make this work," asked the Mayor.

"Well, the deposit has to be a substantial one—somewhere between $3,000 and $10,000 dollars," responded the Judge. "We have already sent Mr. Grigsby to go and make a $5,000 loan deposit into their bank—which they accepted. If it's made as a loan the depositors will have great standing in a court by auguring the fear of not being paid back because of the bank's mismanaging their assets. They will have no defense against us because of the 'Texas Black Code.' Then we ask the court to place the bank in a receivership of another bank to better manage the seized assets. Of course, the perfect person to be the receivership of this is Mr. Grigsby and the bank would be Royall National Bank."

Judge Dent continued, "Mr. Grigsby is well known and trusted by both whites and the Niggers in Anderson County."

Everyone present seemed to be convinced of the scheme. However, Mr. Grigsby questioned whether or not the Board of Directors would agree to such a plan.

It was then, Mr. Malloy, the wealthiest man in Anderson County, stood up and faced Mr. Grigsby. He said, "Half of the money in Royall National Bank belongs to me, and I will remove every dime of it if the bank does not go along with Judge Dent's plan."

Unfortunately, Mr. Grigsby knew Mr. Malloy's threat was real, and if that happened, it would surely bankrupt Royall National Bank within a month's time. So, Mr. Grigsby agreed to go along with the scheme.

Silence gripped the room. "It's time for a vote, gentlemen," Chairman Grigsby stated. The vote was calculated—six said, "Yes," and two said, "No," in favor of taking Farmers and Citizens Savings Bank's assets through the court using the 'Texas Black Code' laws. Then a meeting was scheduled and

Mr. Grigsby met with Judge Dent privately in his chambers at the courthouse where they started to work on the details.

It was only two weeks later that Mr. Grigsby filed a lawsuit in Judge Dent's court on behalf of Royall National Bank and presented the lies that they had come up with that the Farmers and Citizens Savings Bank was mismanaging their funds, which would put their depositors and creditors at risk of never getting their money back. Grigsby argued that the best way to handle this and to solve this crisis was to place the bank in receivership under his authority.

Of course, since this had already been previously arranged, the Judge granted him his request and the receivership of all of Farmers and Citizens Savings Bank's assets went to Mr. Grigsby for Royall National Bank.

The sheriff and deputies came into the Farmers and Citizens Savings Bank during the middle of the day and ordered everyone out of the bank. The doors were then padlocked for no future entry.

Chapter 5

MEETING AT THE "SQUARE"

In 1924, Birdie's mother, Louisiana, passed away. This was devastating for her because she was very close to her mother.

Then, in May 1926, Aunt Birdie received a frantic phone call from her father. He urged her to come back home to Palestine as soon as possible … the bank he had helped to establish and where Aunt Birdie was a major shareholder was having an emergency board meeting. The bank was undergoing a hostile and an illegal takeover by the country's largest white bank in Palestine, the Royall National Bank.

Birdie boarded the next train to Texas and arrived the following day around 7:00 p.m. Immediately she felt the change. Things seemed different in Palestine. She didn't quite know what to make of it. Her father picked her up at the train station. She had never seen him so upset and angry. During the ride to the "Square" to attend the emergency board meeting, her father tried to explain what was happening.

He said that the old man, Mr. Grigsby, who had been the runner for the Royall National Bank from the time he was 12 years old, had gone to meet with the corrupt, Judge Dent.

This meeting had taken place in the judges' private chambers. The result of this meeting was to declare that the Farmers and Citizens Savings Bank was insolvent and unable to pay its account holders and creditors. Already angry, this made him even more furious, shouting, "This is a damn lie ... we have over $90,000 cash in the bank and hundreds of acres of land."

He briefly settled down some and began to explain what had happened in the previous weeks before yesterday's final court decision had been made. He said, "There have been rumors for some time that because of the drought and that the season they were currently in had even been worse than the year before that the Royall National Bank was about to go under. Many of their depositors and customers were large cotton farmers, and they were going belly up—not able to pay their notes. "In fact," he continued, "just last week the bank had to foreclose on old man Davis's family farm. That farm had been in their family for over 100 years," he said.

Furious again, he shouted, "After 26 years of operating, they now say we can't manage our own money and properties." He pounded his fist on the steering wheel. Then he continued to give Bertha the events that led up to the court's decision.

"Now you can understand the urgency in why I needed to notify all of the members of Farmers and Citizens Savings Bank," said Allison. Bertha did understand because he was the largest depositor and had the most to lose.

Bertha and her father arrived at the "Square" to attend the emergency board meeting. There were people everywhere. The word got out quickly that Farmers and Citizens Savings Bank was holding an emergency Town Hall meeting to explain to their depositors what was happening to their money and assets because of this illegal takeover.

Unfortunately, rumors were already circulating that the Farmers and Citizens Savings Bank's board members had stolen their money and property. Naturally, the depositors wanted answers. And why wouldn't they have been upset after the Palestine Daily Herald printed what they did? Allison handed her the newspaper and she read the following:

PALESTINE DAILY HERALD May 4, 1926

Negro Bank In Hands Of Receiver Was An Old Bank

Farmers & Citizens Bank, a private banking institution was placed in the hands of a receiver this morning.

The bank was organized some 17 years and did business among the colored population in this city and county. The bank officers state that declining deposits and inability to realize on their assets are the causes of the bank failure.

On the application of some of the depositors to Judge Ben. F. Dent of the District Court of this county for the appointment of a receiver to take over the affairs and assets of the bank for the protection of the depositors, the court appointed Mr. Jack F. Grigsby as the receiver, with power and authority to immediately take over all of the assets of the bank and administer the same in the interest of the creditors. Mr. Grigsby has entered into a bond as required by the court and has qualified as a receiver and has taken charge of the bank's assets.

He has a long and wide experience in banking affairs, having been connected with the Royall National Bank, one of the largest banking institutions in this section of the state and it is felt by all interested parties that Mr. Grigsby will be able to work out the affairs of this institution and realize on its assets to the very best advantage to all concerned.

Mr. Grigsby requests all the depositors in the bank to call on him and bring their bank books to be balanced and verified, and at the same time make any inquiry they desire relative to the affairs of the bank and he will gladly give all of the depositors full information on the situation.

From a brief review and analysis of the assets and securities owned by the bank, it is believed by the receiver and the managing officers of the bank that the depositors will be ultimately paid a very substantial amount of their deposits with a strong probability that they will be paid in full.

Birdie and her dad, Allison, were escorted through the crowd to the back office where several of the board members had already gathered. They wanted to speak with them before they addressed the confused and angry crowd. The atmosphere among the board members was chaotic. Several contentious conversations about who was at fault were already taking place.

Allison immediately called the meeting to order. Everyone settled in, and they began to discuss what to do about the illegal takeover of their bank, and what should they tell their angry depositors and stockholders, who were now waiting outside.

Again, all they had to go on was what was presented in the court when Royall National Bank brought the charges against them. So much of what was being discussed now was hear-say or rumors that were circulating around town between the whites and the Blacks. Many of the board members admitted to hearing the same rumors Allison had heard.

However, their main focus was how to legally address the theft and reclaim their bank and its customers' assets. They all agreed that the local courts offered them no legal remedy, for they knew old Judge Dent hated Blacks and was more than likely in on it. They discussed taking the matter to the Federal courts.

Allison, who had a history of violence, suggested they take up arms and go and retake what was rightfully theirs. The board rejected Allison's armed violence plan because one of the Black depositors, who had already tried to go to the bank and get his money back, had been tarred and feathered by some angry white men. This act of cruelty was to bring fear to discourage any other action from the Blacks who were involved.

They continued to seriously discuss their options, even if it included bringing Federal attention to the crime. However, a decision was not agreed upon at that time as to their next step.

The board then addressed how and what they were going to tell their angry depositors and investors, who were angrily waiting outside for answers. The local newspaper had released a statement earlier in the day stating that Farmers and Citizens Savings Bank was in receivership of Royall National Bank because Farmers and Citizens Savings Bank was mismanaging its depositors' funds. Naturally, this news had the depositors confused and angry, for many of them had their life savings, money, and property tied up in the Farmers and Citizens Savings Bank. And … after all, shouldn't you be able to believe the newspapers do their job to find out the truth before they publish? Yeah, that's another whole story now isn't it?

The board addressed the crowd and with no uncertain terms stated that what happened to Farmers and Citizens Savings

Bank was a hostile takeover of their money, and land, and they were going to fight it with every ounce of strength they had and with the help of Almighty God to get back every penny and the property that was stolen, even if they had to go all the way to the Supreme Court.

Many in the crowd cheered, but others were still worried and scared for the future of their families and their children.

Later, the Moody Manuel of Investments showed the following information regarding the money taken from Farmers and Citizens Savings Bank by Royall National Bank. In 1926, Royalle's total deposits were $1,557,722.00. After the illegal takeover, in 1927, their total deposits showed $2,273,563.00. I guess their plan worked!!!

MOODY'S MANUAL OF INVESTMENTS

STATEMENT OF CONDITION, AS OF DEC. 31

RESOURCES:	1927	1926
ans and discounts	$701,741	$748,167
S. bonds (circulation)	100,000	100,000
ther U. S. Govt. bonds, etc.	141,974	105,681
anking house, fixtures, etc.	104,041	94,558
onds, securities, etc.	1,250	1,250
ederal Reserve Bank stock	9,000	9,000
Collateral call loans	850,000	225,000
Bills of exchange	73,055	10,451
Cash and due from banks	292,502	263,595
Total	$2,273,563	$1,557,722

Chapter 6

WILL JUSTICE PREVAIL?

For years, the leaders of the Farmers and Citizens Savings Bank petitioned the state courts and politicians for help. No one would agree to even hear their case. Ten years later, Birdie moved back to Palestine from Chicago. The community she once lived in and loved was devastated. Many of the farmers had lost their farms. The "Square" was a ghost town, the stores and cafes were closed. Local schools and colleges that had been supported by the bank were also closed. Those who could leave Palestine in search of a better life, had left.

I remember thinking about watching Aunt Bertha as she laid the pictures and documents back into the box. She had looked up at me and stated ..."I wanted you to know how life was for me, my family, and the Blacks who lived in Palestine, Texas, at that time. I vowed to my father and those families whose lives were destroyed by what happened to their bank on May 3, 1926, that I would dedicate my life to finding out the truth and to restore to their families what was taken.

"I'm sorry to say that it has been over 50 years now, and hundreds of court battles have taken place, but not one penny or property has been returned to its rightful owners. I am old now, and I can't do things like I once did." She ended the conversation by stating, "We felt alive and free back then. We were experiencing the glory of being an American citizen, the independence of controlling your destiny. We were Americans."

My husband, Billy, and I became her caretakers when she fell ill that year. It was eight months later that she passed away. As executives of her estate, it was our responsibility to go through her papers and property to determine what to do with her assets. She was no longer married.

As we were going through her closet, I came across that old silver box that Aunt Birdie had initially brought out to show me the summer before when she shared the stories about her father, her lifestyle, and the bank they had invested in in Palestine, Texas.

I started to share with Billy about the stories Aunt Birdie had told me that hot summer day, but he just brushed it off as one of Aunt Birdie's old fables that she liked to tell ... most of which is probably not true he thought. I figured he was right and set the box in the pile of items that were marked for donations. I thought if the box was cleaned up, it would make a nice gift for someone. So, I sat it aside and continued to go through all the items that were stored in Aunt Birdie's closet.

After cleaning and preparing the silver box to be donated to Goodwill the next day, I went to bed. That night, I wrestled and tossed through many unfamiliar dreams. One of the dreams that stood out the most to me was where waves of black oil, were washing over me, and at times overtaking me. I woke up because of all the restless dreams. I woke Billy up to tell him about the dreams, but he told me to try and go back to sleep, but I couldn't.

I got up to fix some coffee and to reflect on the weird dreams I was having. As I sipped on my coffee a very bright sparkle of light caught the corner of my eye. I noticed it was the Sun rising through the window, reflecting off of the silver box I had cleaned the night before. The Sun's reflection shining off of the box was as if a majestic aura was surrounding it. I couldn't take my eyes off of it. It was as if this box was speaking a message that I needed to hear.

I went over and picked the box up, and it was as if it was the first time that I had seen it. Cleaning the box the night before revealed such intricate details that truly only the sunlight could have revealed. My mind immediately went back to the day Aunt Birdie told me all those stories of her family and what had happened at their bank in Palestine, Texas.

I decided to keep the box for myself, and I began to place all of the pictures and paperwork back inside of it. However, when I picked up the Farmers and Citizens Savings Bank

Stock Certificate to put it back into the box, I could not put it down. It was then that I remembered what Aunt Birdie had told me. She had stated how she vowed to her father that she would do whatever it took to reveal the truth of what happened to Farmers and Citizens Savings Bank and to restore the glory back to Palestine.

Holding the stock certificate I could feel the power of Aunt Birdie's words and in some strange way the same commitment of finding out the truth being transferred to me. For several minutes I could not move. It was as if I was being pulled into that time of history to see firsthand the Black people of Palestine, moving and operating with such purpose, dignity, and class. Then—suddenly it ended.

It was at this point I was determined to discover the truth behind the rumors Aunt Birdie had told me about concerning the Farmers and Citizens Savings Bank.

However, the biggest question I now faced was, "How could I do this?"

Farmers & Citizens Savings Bank

(UNINCORPORATED)

CAPITAL STOCK, ~~$25,000.00~~ 50000.00

This Certifies that Birdie Gardner is the owner of Eighty-Eight Shares of the Capital Stock of

Farmers & Citizens Savings Bank, Palestine, Texas

FULL PAID AND NON-ASSESSABLE–NEGOTIABLE

transferable only on the Books of the Corporation by the holder hereof in person or by Attorney on surrender of this Certificate properly endorsed.

In Witness Whereof, the said Corporation has caused this Certificate to be signed by its duly authorized officers and to be sealed with the Seal of the Corporation this day of Mar. 1 1920

[illegible] Cashier E. W. Griggs [illegible]

Shares $100 Each.

Reagan Museum Palestine, Texas

Chapter 7

THE FIRST TRIP TO PALESTINE

I thought the first thing I should do was to authenticate the Farmers and Citizens Savings Bank's stock certificate. So, I got the phone number for the New York Stock Exchange, and I called them. I asked the gentleman who answered the telephone if he could give me some information on the Farmers and Citizens Savings Bank stock. I gave him the stock number and the number of shares that was printed on Aunt Birdie's certificate. He then told me that the number I had given him did not belong to Aunt Birdie. It was now in the name of Sarah Gunn. She was the individual who owned that stock certificate.

I preceded to tell him that I had the original stock certificate in my hand, and that it had not been sold. He told me that he couldn't give me any information on Sarah Gunn's stock certificate. I said, "Thank you," and hung up the phone. I then told Billy, "We need to go to Palestine and find out what happened to that bank."

The day finally came and Billy and I headed to East Texas. It didn't take us long to find it at all. I was filled with excitement and Billy was there, but no noticeable excitement was evident on his face. I was different. I was definitely excited and anyone who saw me would know that I was anxious as well, not sure of what I'd find. Nevertheless, my determination overrode an anxiousness, and I kept focusing on finding out as much information as I could about this bank and the certificate my husband had inherited from his aunt.

My preliminary searching had validated that such a bank existed, but not much more than that. I needed more proof, which would provide me with the closure I needed. After all, Aunt Birdie must have had a reason for holding on to the certificate, even if maybe for sentimental reasons only.

So, the Farmers and Citizens Savings Bank was real, and the certificate at one time had value. So, I kept searching for the closure notification through various Palestine newspapers. Nothing could ease my level of curiosity. This is why I knew I had to go to Palestine. I knew that even in small towns, someone kept the history, and I wanted all the history I could gather.

Of course, I had done some research about the city of Palestine before I just took off to go there. My research pointed to the Reagan Museum, which is called the museum of East Texas Culture. I can still vividly recall the excitement of what could be possible—even though at the time, I had no clue as to what those possibilities would look like.

I wondered aloud, "Did these Black bankers make the museum?" I so desperately wanted them to have done so. But I realized that their lives were in the 1920's, and life was so different for Black people back then. Even those men who were brave and astute enough to start their own businesses and even had the audacity to start their own financial institution, many of their accomplishments were overlooked and not valued as the pioneering efforts that were needed to do so.

We drove up to the museum—a classic renovated, gothic style brick building from the 1920's. I would learn that it had initially been a school house, named after John H. Reagan, until it was closed in 1976. It had been destined to be demolished, but a concerned, caring citizen saved it, and it became the Museum of Culture for East Texas—hopefully the place that held some of the answers I needed. I had to find out what was inside those walls.

Upon arriving and parking, Billy decided to walk around the area, as I left to go inside. His lack of participation didn't bother me at all. After all, this had now become a personal quest. Maybe he didn't want to see me experience the disappointment he was sure I would find. I gathered myself together and walked in.

The museum had a section dedicated to Black history in East Texas, but there was nothing about the Farmers and Citizens Savings Bank, except a copy of a stock certificate that had been owned by Zula Dial. I told the museum guide about the stock certificate I had from Aunt Birdie, but she had no information or knowledge about the bank, and the curator, Mr. Drew Franklin, who would have had some of the answers, wasn't there that day. So, the guide asked if we could leave a copy of the stock certificate I had for Mr. Franklin to see when he came in, and she would contact us with his findings. So, we left a copy of the certificate with her and headed back to Dallas.

After a few weeks, Mr. Franklin called me. I was at work, and it was hard for me to restrain myself from screaming when he started to tell me that he had a copy of the original merger, which showed that Farmers and Citizens Savings Bank had merged with Royal National Bank. I was shocked! Normally, you can't stop me from talking, but that day, this information silenced me.

Just as so many others had thought, I simply assumed that Farmers and Citizens Savings Bank had failed. However, while on the phone with him, I quickly asked him if he would send me a copy of the merger documents. He graciously agreed to do so. I provided him with my address and asked him if I needed to send him any more money for postage, but he didn't respond.

Weeks went by, but nothing came—no phone calls, no notes, nothing. Obviously, something was prohibiting him from being able to keep his word and send me the documents.

At first, I thought that maybe he had become ill or had to leave town on business. I will never be certain of what actually happened. I just knew that he was so nice when we spoke on the phone and that he very quickly agreed to copy them and send me a copy(s), which never came.

After Mr. Franklin cut off all communication with me, I began to wonder what was in those documents that he didn't want me to see. I became even more determined to get my hands on those documents. I thought that if the museum had a copy, surely Royall National Bank would have copies also, so I reached out to Royall National Bank and explained to them that I had a stock certificate from Farmers and Citizens Savings Bank and I wanted to get more details about the merger. They agreed to meet with me to discuss the issue and set up an appointment with Royall National Bank's CEO, Mr. Welty.

Naturally, I wanted to meet with them, so Billy and I left once again to go to Palestine. We arrived early for the meeting. So, we waited in the car, checking out our surroundings. We had heard about so many strange things that had happened to so many Black people who had lived in Palestine that we didn't want to take any chances.

At the time the meeting was to start, I went into the Bank.

Billy stayed in the car. Mr. Welty called me to his office and got right to the point, addressing the Farmers and Citizens Savings Bank stock that I had. The conversation that followed was very well rehearsed. How he answered my questions, and the way he expressed the intricate details of a merger that happened 60 years ago, more than gave me the impression that he had experienced these types of questions before, possibly with other Farmers and Citizens Savings Bank stockholders who were also seeking answers.

He stated that the share of stock that I had was the only piece of stock that was held out that they didn't own. I knew this was true, only because Birdie had told me she had refused to sell them any of her stock. Then, to add insult to injury, he offered to buy back Bertha's stock. In his words, "To take them off of my hands," for fifty cents a share. I was not only mad now, but highly insulted. He could tell by the look on my face this was not going to be acceptable. I declined the offer.

However, I could tell by the look on his face, that he was ready to end the discussion. He looked at me sternly and said, "Go back to Dallas, and forget this ever happened."

During the meeting, he had shown me a court document that showed how Farmers and Citizens Savings Bank had borrowed money from them. He didn't say that they didn't pay it back—he just said that they borrowed it. After this meeting, I burned with more determination to find the truth.

At this point in my journey, I still didn't know what the next move should be. However, I felt an overwhelming desire to return to Palestine to seek out someone from the Black community who would know something about the Farmers and Citizens Savings Bank. I didn't have a clue who to talk to or where to even start in finding someone.

I convinced Billy to take another trip to Palestine. He was under the impression I had an appointment and knew where I was going … the exact opposite was true … I had no idea where I was going. All I knew was that I had to drive back to Palestine to find someone from the Black community who could tell me about Farmers and Citizens Savings Bank.

Royall National Bank

Chapter 8

ANOTHER TRIP TO PALESTINE

When we arrived again in Palestine, Billy began to ask me for the address to where we were going … I didn't say a word. He asked again … again I didn't say a word. Suddenly, he realized what was happening. He shouted, "You don't know where you're going, do you?" The truth was, I didn't have a clue where I was going. He pulled the car over and stopped.

"Marilyn, you brought me all the way out here and you don't have an appointment?" he said, expressing his frustration.

I then said, "I'm sorry, but I just felt led to find someone from the community who might give me some insight into what had actually happened to the Farmers and Citizens Savings Bank. And I knew if they still lived here, they would know and would have heard what actually had happened to the bank."

Shaking his head, he began to drive to the Black section of Palestine. I instructed him to stop near a local convenience store that was just up ahead. I got out and walked up to the front of the store … but looked back at him, hoping he would not leave me.

As people were going in and out of the store, I asked if they knew anything about the Farmers and Citizens Savings Bank, the Black bank that was once in Palestine. No one even knew Palestine had ever had a Black owned bank. Needless to say, I was feeling discouraged and the frustration on Billy's face was growing by the second.

I then approached another lady who was going into the store. I asked her, "Do you know anything about the Farmers and Citizens Savings Bank?"

She said, "I had no idea a bank ever existed in Palestine, BUT I know someone who might know."

The lady pointed me to a house a couple of blocks away—the woman who owned the house was Dorothy Robertson. She then went on to say, "If anybody would know anything about a Black bank in Palestine, it would be Mrs. Dorothy.

As it turned out, Dorothy Robertson had been a freelance writer for the local Palestine newspaper. The lady at the store was right, if anybody in this town would have known anything about life in Palestine, it would have been her.

I rushed back to the car to tell my frustrated husband that I had found the one person I was looking for, and she just lived up the street. Shaking his head, he put the car in motion and began to drive us toward her house … although, the whole time he was saying, "You are losing it, Marilyn … you don't know these people … you are losing it!"

We arrived at a small, well-kept house. I walked up to the front door. I certainly didn't know what to expect. I reached out and rang the doorbell … about 30 seconds went by … no answer. So, I rang it again. I looked back at Billy sitting in the car, who was now just shaking his head.

Then, the door opened slightly and a slim, older woman stood there. Before she could even speak, I introduced myself. I told her what I was seeking. Dorothy opened the door and welcomed me in. It was almost as if she had been expecting me. I looked back at Billy and waved for him to come in, but he just shook his head, and waved for me to go on in.

I followed Dorothy into the house. It was filled with books and magazine articles. As we sat down, she stated, "I have been expecting you."

I began to brief her on my mission to find out the truth about the Farmers and Citizens Savings Bank. I told her about the stories or rumors that Aunt Birdie had previously told me.

Dorothy was well aware of the rumors and actually confirmed her knowledge of my Aunt Birdie, her father, and the extraordinary achievements of some of the Blacks who lived in Palestine. Some of whom had just come straight out of slavery.

Dorothy informed me that she was in the process of preparing nine copies of the shares of Farmers and Citizens Savings Bank's stock, which was owned by the Dial families, to be placed in an historical museum in San Antonio, Texas.

I asked her, "Why aren't these documents of the Farmers and Citizens Savings Bank being put into the Museum of East Texas Culture?"

Dorothy paused—just staring at me—she didn't say a word. After a few uncomfortable moments she then stated, "So, you must have talked to Drew, the museum curator?"

Before I could even answer, she then went on to explain that the reason she was preparing the Farmers and Citizens Savings Bank stock documents for the San Antonio Black History Museum is because the city of Palestine, and the powers that be, did not want to discuss what happened to the most successful Black community's bank of the 20th century.

If they were to tell the truth of what happened to the Black bank of Palestine, they would have to reveal the awful truth of events about how some of its most prominent citizens (the Royalls and Judge Dent) had destroyed the Black community by illegally taking over Farmers and Citizens Savings Bank.

I told her that I did talk to Drew over the telephone, and he had promised me he would mail the documents of the merger between the Royall National Bank and Farmers and Citizens Savings Bank, but he never sent them, and now he wouldn't even return my calls.

Dorothy rolled her eyes and looked at me with that "child please" expression on her face. She went on to say, "He won't be calling you back, and you will never see those original bank merger documents." Then, Dorothy began to paint a true and clear picture of what had happened in the city of Palestine some 60 years ago—how the Royall National Bank then and even now, its heirs were still profiting from what they had done to the Farmers and Citizens Savings Bank.

I asked Dorothy if she could explain to me why some call the action a "takeover" while others referred to it as a "merger?" She went on to tell me her story about what had actually happened. As a reporter for the local newspaper, Dorothy had wanted to do a feature story on the Farmers and Citizens Savings Bank. She was going to call the article, "Straight out of Slavery." It was going to focus on how the Blacks in Palestine created self-sustaining communities that produced a wealthy, educated class of Blacks, even though they had just been released out of slavery.

Dorothy's research revealed what I had also been able to discover about the unique court documents and conflicting bank records from Royall National Bank concerning Farmers and Citizens Savings Bank. According to the court documents, Farmers and Citizens Savings Bank was placed into receivership, based on a trumped-up charge of mismanagement of funds. In the banking world, the goal of receivership is to manage the bank's assets to make sure all of its creditors and depositors are taken care of, and if possible, return the bank back to its original owners.

However, according to the Royall National Bank ledgers, there were also vast oil wells on the property, but the mineral rights had been reserved by Royall National Bank and members of the Royall family.

Dorothy continued to explain that they discovered the land that the Farmers and Citizens Savings Bank owned was saturated in oil, so they had cooked up a phony "receivership" to justify taking (stealing) the oil from its owners. A receivership would place all of Farmers and Citizens Savings Bank's assets under the total control of Royall National Bank, in particular, Mr. Royall and his family.

BUT, again according to the banking rules, you can't have a merger without the consent of the current President of the bank. At that time, we could not find any documents that showed the principal members of Farmers and Citizens Savings Bank ever agreeing to a merger with Royall National Bank.

Dorothy had actually contacted Royall National Bank to see

if they could explain how a court order of "receivership" had been turned into a "merger" without the consent of the owners. She was told by the paper's editor to drop the story and turn over her research. Right then, she knew that she had uncovered the ugly past of Palestine. And as a result of her findings, even though they would not admit it, she was soon let go from the paper. She wasn't given a reason for her termination, but she knew it had to do with the dark secrets of the white bank's illegal actions and the effects it had had in Palestine that she had uncovered.

Soon after, Dorothy decided to start her own local newsletter, focusing on the Black community in Anderson County. Once this was being published and sent out, strange things began to happen to her, and a few months later, her husband was shot and killed. He was actually at their home in the driveway, changing the oil in their car, when he was shot. She had already been receiving threatening mail and phone calls, warning her to watch her back. Unfortunately, the police offered her little help, and to this day her husband's killer has never been caught.

Dorothy turned and looked at me. I couldn't even speak. I was so shocked by the stories she had just told me. Dorothy then very seriously stated, "My advice to you is to get a good lawyer who may discover that millions of dollars are due to the Black families of Palestine from the oil reserves on the land they owned."

What Dorothy had just told me confirmed two things to me—the dreams I had seen when the waves of oil flowed over me and the rumors I had heard about the oil reserves being on that property. I thanked her with a big hug, and with much excitement I told her, "I will find a lawyer as soon as I get back to Dallas."

I then remembered Aunt Birdie telling me that she had been rich, and it was still down there in the bank. However, we could not go and get it. She said that if she tried to go and get her money, they would kill her. I told her that this wasn't true. Maybe, they would do that in the old days, but things had changed, and they couldn't do that now.

However, my opinion began to change. I soon found out that things hadn't changed that much at all. The sad thing was, even to this day, they were still holding onto the depositors and stockholders certificates.

Chapter 9

THE INVESTIGATION BEGINS

I was referred to another lawyer, Mr. Shor, who knew how to "take care of business." In fact, he had even sued the government and won his case. I was very encouraged that he would be able to help me. We met and he wanted $2,500.00 to take the case upfront. I paid him and then he ordered the court documents from the Anderson County clerk regarding the Farmers and Citizens Savings Bank. After he received them, he sent me a letter requesting I come back to his office for a visit. When I got there, he told me he could not take the case and gave me the court document and a partial refund of the money I had already paid him. When I asked him to tell me why he could not help me his response was, "Blacks were just treated like the Indians had been. Their land was just taken, too."

After leaving his office, I was very, very disappointed. It was then I was recommended to go and see another attorney. The last thing I wanted to do was see another attorney. Why would I want to go through this disappointing process again?

However, the one thing that Mr. Shor accomplished was getting the documents from Anderson County so I had proof of some of the transactions that had taken place in the bank. Shortly after he dropped my case, on the 16th day of January 1929, I received the court documents. These documents also showed the building that was owned by the Farmers and Citizens Savings Bank had been sold to J. C. Callier for the amount of $4,000 and each and all of the rights, which included the title, and interest of the Farmers and Citizens Savings Bank of Palestine, Texas, plus all of its original stockholders.

Another individual, J. C. Ritter of Palestine, Texas, purchased the land in the West Palestine Heights addition for $325.00. They conveyed the land and all of the rights, title, and interest of the Farmers and Citizens Savings Bank. I can't tell you how shocking it was to see how the Royall National Bank was selling the stock certificates from the Farmers and Citizen's Savings Bank without them even knowing about it. I wondered at the time if there was ever going to be any justice for the depositors and stockholders of the Farmers and Citizens Savings Bank.

In 1926, the Moody Manual, that kept all the records on banks, showed the Royall National Bank had a total of $1,557,722 on hand, and in 1927 it had increased to $2,273,563. This increased amount was evidence alone that they had taken everything the Farmers and Citizens Savings Bank owned and all the money the depositors and stockholders had invested in the bank for their own benefit.

Royall National Bank had been the corresponding bank for Farmers and Citizens Savings Bank. The corresponding bank for Royall National Bank was Chase Manhattan, NA.NY; Texas American Bank/Fort Worth NA. Fort Worth; Republican Bank, Tyler, Texas; Community Bank Austin NA.

On September 21, 2004, I called Hibernia Bank after I heard that they had bought out Royall National Bank, and I asked who was doing the merger for Royall National Bank. I was told that Charles Allain was doing the merger. I asked if I could meet with him about the merger. He made an appointment for me to come in the following week.

My daughter and I went to Plano to meet with Mr. Allain. After we arrived, we were immediately invited into his office. I had Aunt Birdie's stock certificate with me. I asked if the Farmers and Citizens Savings Bank had merged with Royal National Bank. He confirmed that they had. He then started to do the paperwork to open me an account. He was going to start it out with $50,000. He then called Rita at the main office in New Orleans. She told him she couldn't turn on her computer because they had just had a hurricane. She told him to call her back in a few days. Mr. Allain told me to come back the next week, and he would continue to complete my deposit.

We went back the next week, and he called us into his office. He told us to have a seat, and then he began to apologize. He told us that he couldn't open the account and for me to go and get a lawyer. I asked him what the problem was, but all he could say was, "You need to get a lawyer."

I thanked him, and we left his office. I knew that whatever he had seen in their records was the reason he was not able to help me. I couldn't be sure of what it was. Maybe he just needed some more information. Or, I also wondered if he had seen where Sarah Gunn was now the one listed to get the dividends from the stock.

So, the investigation continued, and I was able to come up with certified documents now that proved the financial condition of the Royall National Bank and the actions that took place. Here are the results.

On May 3rd, 1926, the District Court at Crockett in Anderson County appointed J. F. Grigsby as the receiver for Farmers and Citizens Savings Bank to manage its assets and ensure fair distribution to its creditors and depositors. The bank faced severe financial distress, with less than $2,000 in cash, uncollectible assets, and deposits reduced from $92,295.64 to $23,000 leading to inequitable assets distribution.

The court emphasized the urgency of intervention to prevent further losses. The receiver was empowered to manage assets, collect debts, and initiate legal actions to recover funds. Creditors were authorized to file claims, and the receiver was required to take an oath and provide a bond before assuming duties.

CHAMBERS AT CROCKETT, TEXAS, MAY 3rd, 1926.

On this 3rd day of May, 1926, the above and foregoing petition, which appears to have been duly filed in the District Court of Anderson County, Texas, on May 3rd, 1926, and duly sworn to by the plaintiffs herein, and it appearing to the court from an examination of said petition and the facts alleged therein that it is necessary and to the best interest of the depositors and creditors of said defendant, Farmers & Citizens Savings Bank that a Receiver of all the property and assets of said Bank should be immediately appointed to take charge thereof without notice and that the delay necessary and occasioned by setting the application for receivership in said petition down for hearing will more than likely incur irreparable loss and damage to plaintiffs and probably result in an unequal, unfair and unjust distribution of the assets of said defendant, Farmers & Citizens Savings Bank;

And it further appearing to the Court that J. F. Grigsby of Anderson County, Texas, is a suitable person to act as such Receiver and that he is not disqualified therefor, it is, therefore, ordered, adjudged and decreed by the court that J. F. Grigsby, of Anderson County, Texas, be and he is hereby appointed as Receiver, with full authority and power to immediately take into his possession, custody, control and management all and singular all of the monies, notes, accounts, choses in action, and all other personal property, as well as all real estate and all other assets and property of every character and description of said defendant, Farmers & Citizens Savings Bank, and that he hold, control, administer and manage the same as such Receiver under the direction and power herein given and such as may be hereafter given by the further orders and decrees of this Court, and with full power in him, the said J. F. Grigsby, as such Receiver, to collect and receive all monies due and owing to said defendant and to enforce the payment of all notes, debts and other obligations due and owing to said Bank, to sell, transfer & assign to other parties, said notes, debts & obligations for the face value thereof with interest, without recourse & and to accept and take renewals of any and all notes and other obligations due and owing to said Bank which are past due in order to prevent the same from being barred by the statutes of limitations, provided that such renewals of said indebtedness shall not extend for a period of time that will extend beyond November 1, 1926, unless otherwise ordered by this court, and with full authority in him, the said Receiver,

The plaintiff highlighted the unfair asset distribution and the inaction of the bank's management, which allowed overdue debts to risk becoming barred by the statute of limitations.

They sought a court-supervised solution to prevent further harm and requested a judgement against the bank and its officers for the amounts owed to secure equitable asset management and safeguard the interest of all affected parties.

On November 9, 1926, Mr. Grigsby, receiver for Farmers and Citizens Savings Bank of Palestine, Texas, submitted an inventory of the bank's assets, including notes, mortgages, deeds of trust, and real estate evaluation, although the accuracy of these figures could not be verified. The bank, facing financial difficulties, admitted to the allegations in the case and consented to the foreclosure of a 200-acre lien by Robinson Loan & Mortgage Company to settle part of its debt.

Intervenors, including S.A. Simpson ($302), Joe G. Donaldson ($1.25), and Queen Esther Circle ($0.61), filed pleas for payment of their deposits. They requested the court to order the receiver to pay them the amounts due, as verified by the bank's records and the receiver's statement.

The plaintiffs, consisting of deposits and creditors, outlined the bank's liabilities. They highlighted a demand of $53,000,00, time deposits of $20,709.87, and other debts amounting to $10,000.00.

Individual claims included amounts owed to M.E. Williamson ($816.84), Jim Basley ($726.71), A.S. Davis ($1,597.20), and others, totaling significant liabilities.

The petition described this as a joint-stock company with extensive liabilities to depositors and creditors. The plaintiffs sought a court-supervised resolution to ensure a fair and equitable distribution of assets, including payment of their respective claims.

On May 3, 1926, Robinson Loan & Mortgage Company intervened in the legal case against the Farmers and Citizens Savings Bank, claiming the bank defaulted on a $1,200.00 promissory note from 1921. The note, secured by a lender's lien on a 200-acre tract of land, remained unpaid beyond its due date, with only interest paid up to December 19, 1925.

The Robinson Loan & Mortgage Company asserted that the lien on the land was valid, subsisting, and superior to any other claims against the bank. Despite repeated demands, they failed to settle the debt. The intervenor requested the court to enforce its lien and grant the received, Mr. Grigsby, the authority to manage the bank's assets to ensure payment of the outstanding debt.

The document summarized the proceedings and interventions related to the financial insolvency of the Farmers and Citizens Savings Bank.

Inventory of Assets & Property of the Farmers & Citizens Savings Bank, that have come into the hands of J. F. Grigsby as Receiver of said Bank, under appointment of the District Court of Anderson County, Texas.

File No.	Maker	Security	Date	Int from	[illegible]
66	J.W.Austin	Mtg	1/30/26	10/15/26-10%	$248.21
67	J.W.Austin	Mtg	3/24/26	10/15/26 -10%	66.56
68	G.V.Anderson	Mtg	1/26/26	10/15/26-10%	316.43
69	G.V.Anderson	Mtg	4/20/26	10/15/26-10%	82.50
70	Isaiah Burton	Mtg	2/3/26	10/15/26-10%	83.50
71	John Burton	Mtg	1/11/26	10/15/26-10%	617.18
72	John Burton	Mtg	4/27/26	10/15/26-10%	55.00
73	Grant Barrett	Mtg	2/13/26	10/15/26-10%	165.50
74	J.C & Grant Barrett	Mtg	2/20/26	10/15/26-10%	55.50
75	Charley Benson	Mtg	2/20/26	10/15/26-10%	220.50
76	Ed Benton	Mtg	3/23/26	10/15/26-10%	110.50
77	Ola Mae & Milton Bragg	Mtg	1/26/26	4/28/26-10%	31.50
78	B.F.Brown	Mtg	1/16/26	10/15/26-10%	220.50
79	Harvey Brooks	Mtg	~~2~~/29/26	5/14/26-10%	10.75 ~~10.50~~
80	Ella Baker	Mtg	3/20/26	10/12/26-10%	63.00
81	Collins & Columbus Brown	Mtg	3/23/26	10/15/26-10%	42.30
82	W.M.Brown	Mtg	2/15/26	10/15/26-10%	193.00
*83	Elija L. Carter	Bk.Stock	2/18/26	date-10%	500.00
84	Parks Calhoun	Mtg	4/15/26	mat-10%	15.50
85	Ezell Conoway	Mtg	3/11/26	10/15/26-10%	66.50
86	Fred Daniel	Mtg	4/10/26	Mat-10%	152.22
87	Richard Durham	Mtg	4/20/26	7/14/26-10%	36.50
88	John Darden	Mtg	2/13/26	10/15/26-10%	66.50
89	A.V & R.D.Daniels	~~Mtg~~	4/5/26	11/1/26-10%	79.00
90	S.E.Diggs	~~Mtg~~	4/5/26	6/5/26-10%	25.75
91	J.W.Elmore	bk.Stock	2/1/26	10/15/26-10%	220.00

The document detailed actions by the court, the receiver, and various intervenors, who were seeking repayment of deposits. On February 3, 1927, the court authorized receiver Mr. Grigsby to renew or foreclose on notes and mortgages as needed, take over the mortgaged property with the debtor's consent, and sell assets privately.

131

No. 14,887. 1929-1

M. E. Williamson, et al,) In the District Court of

vs.) Anderson County, Texas,

Farmers & Citizens Savings Bank.) November Term, A. D. 1929.

On this 16th day of January, A. D., 1929, came on to be heard the application of J.F.Grigsby,Receiver, in the above entitled and numbered cause, for an order and authority to sell certain real estate owned by the Farmers & Citizens Savings Bank of Palestine, Anderson County, Texas, which property is hereinafter described, and the Court, after hearing the evidence and facts relative to the market value of said property, is of the opinion that part of Lots 1, 2, 3, and 4, in Block 161, I-GN RR. Co. Addition to the City of Palestine, Texas, and being the building commonly known as the Farmers & Citizens Savings Bank building, is reasonably worth $4000.00 and that $4000.00 is a fair price for same and that one J.C.Callier of Anderson County, Texas, has offered to pay the sum of $4000.00 cash for said property.

It is, therefore, ordered and directed by this Court that the said J.F.Grigsby, Receiver, asforesaid, make an instrument conveying said property to the said J.C.Callier, without warranty as to title or any other encumbrances, for a consideration of $4000.00 cash. Said instruments shall convey to J.C.Callier above named all of the right, title and interest of the Farmers & Citizens Savings Bank of Palestine, Texas, and each and all of its stockholders as such in and to the property above described.

Ben F. Dent
Judge Presiding.

Page #3.

Land Company's Addition to the City of Palestine, Texas, is reasonably worth $250.00 and $250.00 is a fair price for same, and that one T.C.Ritchey of Palestine, Anderson C ounty, Texas, has offered to pay $250.00 cash for said lot. It is, therefore, ordered and directed by this Court that the said J.F.Grigsby, Receiver, make an instrument conveying said property to the said T.C.Ritchey, without warranty as to title or any other encumbrances, for a consideration of $250.00.

And also Lots 2, 3, 4, 6, and 7 in Block A, and also Lots 1, 2, 3, 4, and 5 in Block B; Lots 1, 2, 3, 4, 5, and 6 in Block C; Lots 6, 7 and 10 in Block D; Lots 4, 5, 6, 7, in Block E; also lots 9 and 10 in Block F, and lots 1 and 2 in Block G, all in West Palestine Heights Addition and being twenty-seven lots in all, all of which lots are located and situated in what is known as West Palestine Heights Addition to the City of Palestine, Texas, are reasonably worth $325.00 and $325.00 is a fair price for same, and that one T.C. Ritchey of P alestine, Anderson County, Texas, has offered to pay $325.00 cash for said lots. It is, therefore, ordered and directed by this Court that the said J.F.Grigsby, Receiver, make an instrument conveying said property to the said T.C. Ritchey, without warranty as to title or any other encumbrances, for a consideration of $325.00. Said instruments shall convey to the several parties above named all of the right, title and interest of the Farmers & Citizens Savings Bank of Palestine, Texas, and each and all of its stockholders as such in and to the property above described.

Judge Presiding.

Mr. Grigsby was also directed to settle any outstanding taxes that were owed to the state of Texas, Anderson County, and the City of Palestine.

Several intervenors folded pleas for repayment of funds that had been deposited with the bank prior to its receivership. Claims included amounts owed to individuals such as John Rhodes ($170.00), Fanny Rhodes ($145.60). Additional intervenors, including: Irene Harrison ($3.85), Willie Harrison ($59.03), and Willie May Harrison ($200.00 and $300.00 vie certificate of deposit), sight payment of their deposits and accrued interest.

Other intervenors, such as Mrs. A.M. Franklin ($94.75), Wesle Tubbs ($28.97), J. D. Tubbs ($63.33), and Cynthia Smith ($62.49), emphasized that they were depositors and creditors, but not stockholders. They requested that the court prioritize the repayment to depositors before any funds were given to the stockholders.

The proceedings reflected ongoing efforts to manage the bank's liabilities, with the court and the intervenors, who were seeking equitable resolution for the depositors and creditors, while addressing the bank's debts and assets under the receiver's administration.

The document lists further claims from numerous depositors and creditors of Farmers and Citizens Savings Bank, detailing amounts held at the time the bank was placed under receivership.

Intervenors, including individuals and organizations, sought court orders for repayment of their deposit, ranging from small sums to larger amounts, such as $1,164.70 for A. B. Caldwell and $512.26 for Marie White. They requested prioritization of depositors over stockholders and urged the receiver to manage assets to ensure equitable replacement.

On December 18, 1926, the District Court of Anderson County authorized J. F. Grigsby to distribute a 15% dividend to non-stockholders, depositors, and creditors with approved claims to maximize returns, the receiver proposes accepting mortgage property from willing debtors, selling the bank's assets, and negotiating tax compromises. The court also approved extending or settling certain debts, but restricted payments to stockholders or unresolved creditors.

There were numerous amounts of land that Mr. Grigsby had access to, but I couldn't find the deeds filed in the courthouse. By him not filing the deeds, there is no way to prove who owned the land that was taken.

Chapter 10

RAILROAD COMMISSIONER'S REPORT

As I was sitting, wondering what was going to be my next move, I was just amazed at what I had seen and heard. It was beyond belief how inconsiderate these people had been. I could clearly see how unfair and unjust they had treated the depositors and stockholders—all of it was so wrong. And to think that the reason this happened was because of the color of one's skin, is still devastating to the mind. Taking over the bank would have been one thing, but why would this have needed to be any different than when they previously merged with the other five white banks?

The truth is ... it shouldn't have been any different. If they had obeyed the law and done what was needed, none of this would have happened. They could have still saved Royall National Bank, and at the same time, the rightful owners of Farmers and Citizen's Savings Bank would have maintained their money, stocks, and land that officially and legally belonged to them.

Then I just felt led to look through the court documents again. While looking through them, I found one document dated

April 19, 1940. It had a good description of the land that was sold, and it indicated that Mr. Grigsby was the receiver for the Farmers and Citizens Savings Bank (reserving and excepting from said deeds all the oil, gas and other minerals that may be in or under said real estate, all rights incident there to including the right of ingress and egress.)

On this 19th day of April 1940, came on to be heard the report of J. F. Grigsby, as Receiver of the Farmers & Citizens Savings Bank, of the sale of the real estate hereinafter described made in obedience to the order of this Court made and entered on [illegible] 1940.

And it appearing to the Court that said report of sale has been filed and docketed in the manner and for the time required by law; and it further appearing, upon examination and the evidence herein, that said sale was fairly made, and in conformity with law, and that said real estate brought a fair price; and it further appearing that J. H. Coly became the purchaser of said real estate at private sale, for the sum of [illegible]; that said sale ought to be confirmed, and that said real estate is described as follows, towit:

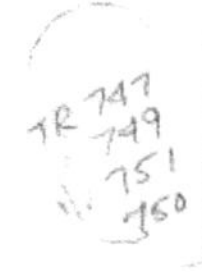

All that certain lot, tract or parcel of land, lying being and situated in the County of Anderson, and State of Texas, a part of the Alfred Benge League and described as follows:

Beginning at the N. W. corner of a 246 acre tract and about 745 vrs. West of the E. B. line of the said league in Caddo Creek; Thence West with the Creek 1805 vrs. to the division line dividing the league into two parts; Thence South with the division line 1990 vrs. to the S. B. line of the league; Thence East 1805 vrs. to the S. W. corner of the said 246 acres; Thence North with the West line of said 246 acres to the place of beginning.

Containing [illegible] acres of land [illegible] and being the same land sold to the said Elbert [illegible] by [illegible], by deed dated March [illegible], and recorded [illegible] 43, Anderson County Deed [illegible] hereby made for further description. The part hereby conveyed and intended to be conveyed being four hundred and fifty six (456) acres off of the west side of the above described land, and being more particularly described in a deed from the surviving wife of Elbert Donnell, [illegible] Farmers & Citizens Savings Bank, dated November 28, [illegible] and recorded in Vol. [illegible] page [illegible] of the Anderson County Deed Records.

IT IS THEREFORE ORDERED, ADJUDGED AND DECREED by the Court, that said sale be and the same is in all respects approved and confirmed; and that said report of sale be recorded

This document only confirms what all they actually stole from the stockholders, investors, and other depositors. After I saw this, I felt that it may be worthwhile to go to Austin, Texas, to visit the Railroad Commission to see if anyone was or had been drilling on that tract of land.

So, we left the next day to drive to Austin. On our way there, we began to plan how we were going to celebrate this great find. What if there really was oil on that land? Especially, since Mr. Grigsby had already reserved all the oil, minerals and natural gas that was under the soil. What a relief it would be if maybe everyone was finally going to start to get the money from the investment they had made years ago.

When we arrived at the Railroad Commission, we asked at the first desk we approached, "Where do we go to find out who was and is still drilling on these acres?" They directed us to the floor where the maps would be available to show us this information. There was a gentleman at the desk, and we asked him if he could tell us if someone was drilling on this property. He took the paper and left the area. It didn't take him but a few minutes to return. He then told us that the Hunt Oil Company was the one who was drilling on that particular tract of land, but we would have to go to the Hunt Oil Company ourselves for the specific information we needed on exactly how many wells were being drilled. We thanked him. We were so excited. We hurried to the car and started our return trip back to Dallas.

When we got back, I went to the Hunt Oil Company and spoke to the receptionist, Alexia Easton, who greeted us when we got there. I asked her if she could tell us how many wells were being drilled on this 656 acres of land. She said she would have to research it, and she would get back with us. She asked for a copy of the court document to do the research.

After about a month had passed, we received a letter from Mrs. Easton. She indicated that it appeared that the land covered oil wells on tracts 849, 850, 851, 852 and possibly 951, and 853. There were also four tracts that she wrote on the court document; those tracts were 747, 749, 751, and 750.

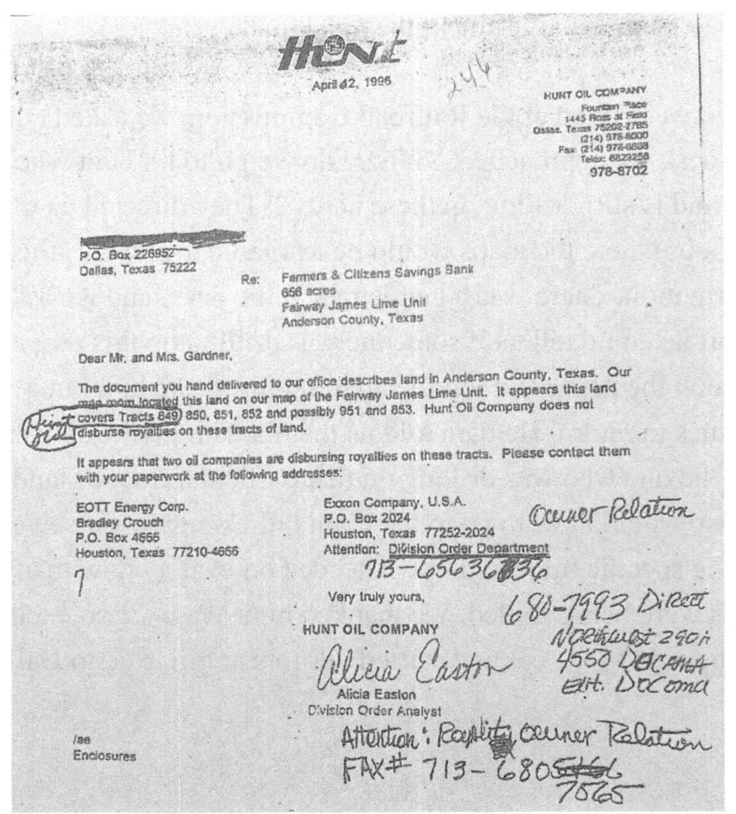

HUNT

April 12, 1996

HUNT OIL COMPANY
Fountain Place
1445 Ross at Field
Dallas, Texas 75202-2785
(214) 978-8000
Fax: (214) 978-8888
Telex: 6829258
978-8702

P.O. Box 226952
Dallas, Texas 75222

Re: Farmers & Citizens Savings Bank
656 acres
Fairway James Lime Unit
Anderson County, Texas

Dear Mr. and Mrs. Gardner,

The document you hand delivered to our office describes land in Anderson County, Texas. Our map room located this land on our map of the Fairway James Lime Unit. It appears this land covers Tracts 849, 850, 851, 852 and possibly 951 and 853. Hunt Oil Company does not disburse royalties on these tracts of land.

It appears that two oil companies are disbursing royalties on these tracts. Please contact them with your paperwork at the following addresses:

EOTT Energy Corp.
Bradley Crouch
P.O. Box 4666
Houston, Texas 77210-4666

Exxon Company, U.S.A.
P.O. Box 2024
Houston, Texas 77252-2024
Attention: Division Order Department

Very truly yours,

HUNT OIL COMPANY

Alicia Easton
Division Order Analyst

/ae
Enclosures

I was then advised that if I wanted to know more about these tracts of land that I would have to go to Kilgore, Texas. As it turns out, Kilgore houses all the information regarding the oil wells in East Texas.

Our next trip was soon planned and off to Kilgore we went. My mother and father decided to take the trip with me. Even though I had already been to the Railroad Commissioner's office in Austin, the reason I needed to go to the Kilgore office was because the records of the breakdown of the wells were kept there. Plus, I would be able to see who was actually receiving money from the oil wells that were currently being drilled there.

I took the court documents that I had gotten from the Hunt Oil Company into the Railroad commissioner's office. These documents showed the tracts and the numbers of the wells that Hunt was drilling.

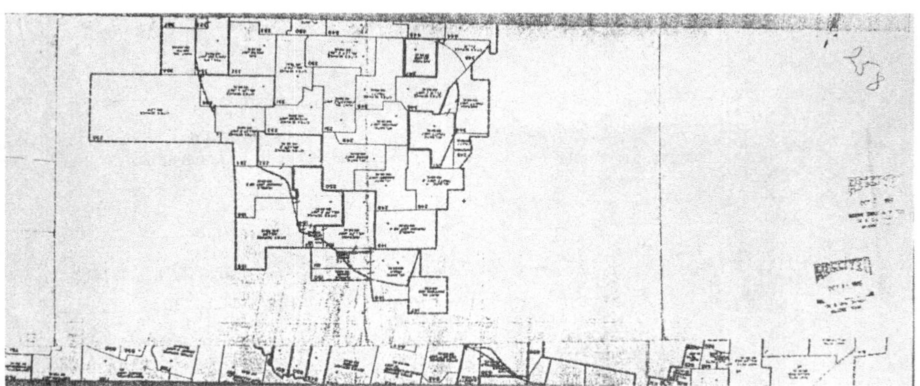

Form H-7
(Eff. 3/1/68)

RAILROAD COMMISSION OF TEXAS
OIL AND GAS DIVISION

FRESH WATER DATA FORM

Date: November 29, 1995

1. RRC District: 6	2. Field Name (as per current proration schedule): Fairway (James Lime) Unit
3. County: Anderson & Henderson	4. Reservoir (into which fresh water is to be injected): James Lime
5. Operator: Hunt Oil Company	
6. Lease Name(s) and RRC No(s). (on which fresh water is to be injected): Fairway (James Lime) Unit (04853)	
7. Name of Fresh Water Formation or Source: Wilcox	8. Depth to Top of Fresh Water Formation (Feet): 458' RKB (-101' SS)
9. Gross Thickness of Fresh Water Formation (Feet): ± 800'	10. Net Thickness of Fresh Water Formation (Feet): 125' (Avg perf'd interval)
11. Total Number of Acres in Project Area where Applicant has Exclusive Use of Fresh Water Rights for Subject Project. Include Land Description. (Also furnish plat. See "Required Attachments" on back.): 22,738	
12. Volume of Recoverable Fresh Water-in-Place beneath Applicant's Water Rights Acreage (Barrels): 2 MMM STB	13. Rate of Recharge of Fresh Water Formation beneath Subject Water Rights Acreage (Barrels/Day): 29,200 (see attached)
14. Total Volume of Fresh Water to be Used in Injection Project (Barrels): 94 MM STB	15. Fresh Water Withdrawal Rates for Project (Barrels/Day): 8,000

16. Other Uses and Withdrawal Rates in Project Area for the same Fresh Water Formation or Source

USES (Specify each.)	RATES (Barrels/Day)
Fairway Gas Plant Cooling	2700

17. Names of and Distances to Municipal Water Supplies Utilizing Same Fresh Water Formation or Source (within 20 mile radius)

CITY/TOWN	DISTANCE AND DIRECTION
Frankston	Partially within Unit boundaries
~~Athens~~	~~18 miles NW~~

18. Name of Shallowest Salt Water or Brackish Water Supply Zone	19. Depth of Shallowest Salt Water or Brackish Water Supply Zone (Feet)	20. Rate of Salt Water or Brackish Water Available from All Sources for Project (Barrels/Day)
Woodbine	± 5000'	± 34,000

(OVER)

Chapter 11

ANOTHER ATTORNEY?

So, as usual, I began to search for another attorney. Someone referred me to Mr. Izen, Jr., who had an office in Corsicana, Texas. I called his office and made an appointment. So, as it was my pattern, I arrived early for the appointment. I waited for the legal assistant to come back into the office. When he arrived, I took the box of court documents to his office, and he began to go over some of the documents. He said that he would give them to the lawyer in Houston, Texas. He gave me his card, so I could follow up with him.

When I hadn't heard from Mr. Izen after several months' time, I was a bit concerned. Then, I received a phone call from him. He wanted me to come to Houston to see him in his office. I agreed. When I arrived at his office, the receptionist asked me to have a seat and said he would call me back to his office shortly.

When I was able to meet with him personally, he told me that he had been a candidate in an election for a position in Washington, D.C., and if he would have gotten that position, he was going to take my case. However, since he didn't win the election, he could not take my case. Then to my surprise, he offered me $300,000.00 to purchase the stock certificate from me. Of course, I rejected the offer. I thanked him, went back to my car, and drove back to Dallas.

ıail - Fwd: Marilyn Oliver's Bank Stocks Page 3

This communication is sent to you at [redacted] request, and he states as follows:

"As discussed by telephone, enclosed is evidence of 88 shares of stock owned by Marilyn Oliver of Texas. Ms. Oliver received this stock as part of a divorce settlement in the early or mid 90's. She was offered approximately $300,000.00 for the stock approximately twenty years ago. We believe the stock is now in the name of Capital One. Enclosed is a chronological listing of all the successor banks ending in Capital One and the dates of merger of each of the banks.

To compound the problem further, the stock certificates, the originals of which are owned by Ms. Oliver, are purportedly owned by Sara Gunn. However, as you can see from the enclosures, Ms. Oliver has been given documents from a financial service entity listing her name as the owner of the stocks.

I need to know from you, if possible, whether the stock certificates she owns are in fact still viable and translate into stock ownership in Capital One. If you need other information, please advise immediately."

What a waste of time. He had me come all the way to Houston to tell me he wasn't going to represent me? AND he thought I would accept his low-ball offer to buy my stock? How do these people make it and pass the bar exam?

So, I'm back in the same rut—trying to find an attorney to help me. I had another attorney who was referred to me from Dallas. I talked with him and hired Mr. Youngblood to help me find out what had happened to the property. He told me that he was going to hire someone to research the land for me. He hired Mr. Pitman to go to Palestine. After his finding, he sent me the different transactions that had taken place before and after Mr. Grigsby had become the receiver of the Farmers and Citizens Savings Bank.

According to the document that Mr. Pitman found, J. F. Grigsby had reserved all the minerals on the 656 acres of land. Mr. Pitman said that there was more property that had been owned by the depositors and stockholders that Mr. Grigsby and the Royall family had put into their own names. He volunteered to go back and pull those deeds for me, if I wanted him to. I thanked him for the information, but told him, "Not at this time."

A few weeks later, after I had had a chance to think about it, I called him and told him that I wanted him to do the research for me. He seemed to be a little nervous and maybe even scared. He told me I could go and get it myself. He explained that I had all the information I needed. He had written the numbers on the bottom of the page. I told him that I was going to pay him, but he refused any money and told me to go and pull them myself. He stated again that the numbers I needed were on the bottom of the page.

I thanked him and hung up the phone, realizing this was just one more time that someone or something had tried to stop any further investigation on my part.

Mr. Youngblood, the attorney I had reached out to, had previously written a letter to the Hunt Oil Company regarding my claim for the mineral/oil rights. On September 30, 1997, Mr. Youngblood received a letter from Mr. Mitchell, who was with the Hunt Oil Company. The letter stated Mr. Grigsby, the receiver of the Farmers and Citizens Savings Bank, only owned the surface of the estate that was formerly owned by Mr. Cely, who had been another land owner. He stated that Mr. Grigsby intended to convey all of the interest in the land and reserve the oil, gas, and other minerals.

I didn't understand how Mr. Grigsby could reserve the oil, gas, and all the other minerals if the Farmers and Citizens Savings Bank didn't have access to it. Mr. Youngblood informed me that Mr. Mitchell had also said in the letter that if I wanted to meet with him, that he would be glad to meet with me. I told Mr. Youngblood, "Yes, I want to have a meeting with him. Can you please set it up for me?"

On the day of the meeting, Mr. Youngblood went with me and my friend, Mrs. Kemp, to the meeting. They took us upstairs to a very large conference room. We sat down, and they offered us a glass of water, which we thanked them for. Then all of these other gentlemen started to come into the conference room. After they sat down, they began to introduce themselves, telling us what positions they held within the Hunt Oil Company. We introduced ourselves to them, Mr. Youngblood as my lawyer, Mrs. Kemp as my friend, and I was the client.

Mr. Mitchell started the meeting by saying that Farmers and Citizens Savings Bank didn't have an interest in that tract of land. I then showed them the paper that I had gotten from Mr.

Pitman's research in Palestine, Texas. I tried to show them where Mr. Grigsby had reserved the oil, gas, and all the other minerals. The Hunt Oil employees asked me if they could see the paper, to know what I was talking about. I said, "Sure," and I passed it across the table to them. They looked at the paper and passed it to the other men sitting around the table.

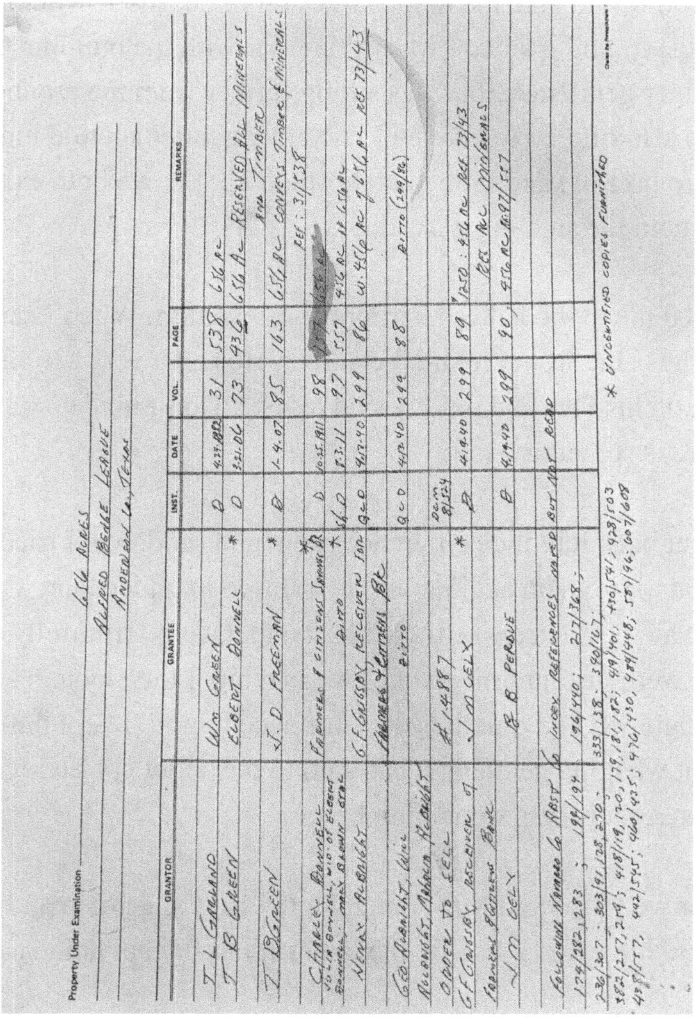

Property Under Examination: 656 Acres, Alfred Benge League, Anderson Co., Texas

GRANTOR	GRANTEE	INST.	DATE	VOL.	PAGE	REMARKS
T L Garland	Wm Green	D	4-27-1882	31	538	656 ac
T B Green	Elbert Donnell *	D	3-21-06	73	436	656 Ac Reserved All Minerals and Timber
T B Green *	J. D Freeman	D	1-4-07	85	163	656 Ac Conveys Timber & Minerals Ref: 31/538
Charley Donnell, Julia Donnell wid of Elbert Donnell, Mary Brown et al *	Farmers & Citizens Savings Bk	D	10-25-1911	98	157	156 Ac
*	Ditto	SWD	8-3-11	97	557	456 Ac
Henry Albright	G.F. Grigsby Receiver for Farmers & Citizens Bk	Q-D	9-17-40	299	86	W. 456 Ac of 656 Ac Ref 73/43
Geo Albright, Wm Albright, Rebecca Albright	Ditto	Q-D	4-17-40	299	88	Ditto (299/86)
Order to Sell	#14887	Dcm 8/1/34				
G F Grigsby Receiver of Farmers & Citizens Bank *	J M Cely	D	4-18-40	299	89	1250: 456 Ac Ref 73/43 Res All Minerals
J M Cely	B B Perdue	D	4-19-40	299	90	456 Ac Ref 97/557

Following Numbered Co Abst & Index References noted but not read
179/282, 283; 199/94; 196/440; 217/368;
236/307; 303/91, 128, 270; 333/138; 380/167
382/257, 259; 418/119, 120, 179, 181, 182; 419/401; 420/541; 428/503
438/157, 442/545; 460/435; 470/430, 484/448; 587/96, 607/608

* Unidentified copies furnished

Once they all had an opportunity to review the paper, they began to respond. They tried to say that Mr. Grigsby wasn't reserving the oil, gas, and minerals. However, this is not what I had been told by Mr. Pitman. After verbally going back and forth with these men, I knew I needed a break. So, I asked them if I could go to the ladies room. An elderly gentleman said he would take me to the ladies room because I wouldn't be able to find it since I wasn't familiar with the building. A younger gentleman that was sitting further from me around the table also offered to take me. The elder gentleman told him he would take me and immediately stood up. So, we both exited the room through big glass doors.

He led me to the ladies restroom and I went in. When I came out, he came from around the corner. He had a very serious look on his face and quietly said to me, "Don't give up on this. There is something to it."

I went back into the conference room and sat down. I tried to explain it to them again, but they refused to understand. Or anyway they acted like they didn't understand. Truthfully, they were just ignoring what I was saying. I then looked at Mr. Youngblood and quietly said, "We need to go!" I kept thinking about what the gentleman had said to me about not giving up because there was something to it.

After we left, I told Mr. Youngblood what the gentleman had said to me when I went to the ladies room. I went home and he went back to his office, but he told me to come to his office the next day, so we could organize my court documents. I did what he said and went to his office the next day. When I arrived, they placed me at a small desk for me to organize the papers. While I was organizing, he had left the office, but came back about an hour later. When he came back, his attitude had totally changed. He said, “I didn’t ask you to read the papers.” He then told me that I could take the papers home with me, which I did. Now, I’m wondering, “Did they get to him also?”

I thought that this was one of the worst injustices that could have been done to the depositors and the stockholders. Because of this disturbing information, I decided to go to the U.S. DEPARTMENT OF JUSTICE, where I spoke to Mr. Savage. I explained to him what had happened to the Farmers and Citizens Savings Bank. He told me to wait a minute because he wanted to get his supervisor to help him. A few minutes later, Mr. Geren, the supervisor, came to the room where Mr. Savage had put us. I explained once again to him what had happened to the Farmers and Citizens Savings Bank and showed him the court documents, which showed how Judge Dent had given the bank to Mr. Grigsby, and everything that the bank owned.

After looking at the court documents, Mr. Geren then said, “Thanks for the history lesson.” He then said, “If you can get someone interested in your case, we would be able to step in." I asked him who I had to go to, but he wouldn't tell me or offer any suggestions. I thanked him and walked out the door.

I don't feel like I should have to go through all of this to claim what is rightfully mine.

Chapter 12

A LAWSUIT IS FILED

However, I had heard about a woman attorney, Miss P. Jackson, who had an office in downtown Dallas. I scheduled an appointment with her. When I arrived at the appointment, they called the attorney assigned to me to let them know that I was there. When the attorney came out, I was surprised to see that she was a Black woman. I didn't think this would be who they would choose to represent me considering the type of case that I was bringing to them for help, especially because of the racial discrimination I was already experiencing.

Miss Jackson came to the reception desk and asked me to come to her office. When I went to the office and explained and showed her the court documents that I had, she didn't seem to be surprised about what had happened to the Farmers and Citizens Savings Bank. She told me that she would look into it and get back with me. She was going to look to see what she could find in the office. I told her I doubted if she would find anything because it was hard for me to find anything about the bank. She said, "Don't be surprised; there is a lot of stuff here in this office." I left feeling relieved that at least she would and could relate to the feelings of discrimination regarding my case.

After a couple of weeks, Miss Jackson called me and told me that I had enough money that I could go into the Royall National Bank and start hiring and firing people. However, I knew that would be something that I would not be able to do. She said this because of the amount of money that I should be entitled to within the bank.

After a couple of months of her seeking the amount of money that I was entitled to, she was so excited that it made me get more excited about the amount of money I should have already received.

A few weeks later, I received another call from Miss Jackson. She needed to meet with me again, but she didn't want to meet in her office. So, we met at the public library. As soon as we sat down, she said, "I will not be able to take your case any longer." At that moment she handed me the court records/documents I had given her. She told me to file a lawsuit about the Farmers and Citizens Savings Bank, and to find another lawyer to take my case. She also told me how to file the lawsuit.

I did exactly what she told me to do. I also continued to look for another lawyer.

Miss Jackson went on to say that I would have to write a book in order to get my money because they didn't intend to pay the original stockholders. I knew what she was telling me was the truth. In some ways, I guess I had felt this was the problem all along. Royall National Bank continued to look over the people who had owned the original stock certificates. My question again was, "If the Farmers and Citizens Savings Bank had gone under, why did it take them over 20 years to liquidate?" I thanked her and took my documents and left the Dallas Library. I immediately went downtown and filed the lawsuit. At this point I felt it might be my last resort.

92-12047

FILED
92 OCT 5 PM 4:28
IN DISTRICT COURT

JUDICIAL DISTRICT

October 5, 1992

TEXAS

DEPUTY

Billy J. Gardner
Marilyn Gardner
James G. Dial
C. C. Dial
Vera Selica Dial
William Tyree Dial
Julia R. L. Dial
G. A. Dial
Zula B. Dial
Plaintiff

Defendant Royall National Bank/Royall Financial Corporation, 519 N. Sycamore Palestine, Texas 75081.

Billy J. Gardner, Marilyn Gardner.

On May 10, 1926 Farmers & Citizen Saving Bank merged with Royall National. Both parties reside in Texas.

On or about May 10, 1926, defendant converted to his own use ten bonds of the Farmers & Citizen Saving Bank Stock.

The value in access of $100,000 dollars, the property of plaintiff.

Wherefore plaintiff demands judgement against defendant in the sum of access 100,000 dollars, interest, dividend and cost's as the court see fit.

Marilyn Gardner
Marilyn Gardner
4433 N. Story #157
Irving, Tx 75038
570-7842

After I filed the lawsuit, Mr. Greco, another reputable attorney was referred to me. I made an appointment and went to his office with the documents he would need. At our meeting, I began to share with him about what Mr. Franklin from the museum in Palestine had told me. They did have a copy of the original merger. I also told him that I had met with Mr. Welty from the Royall National Bank, and he had told me that they had taken over the bank, and then he had bought out all of the stock certificates from the Farmers and Citizens Savings Bank, except for those that Bertha had owned. Mr. Greco took my case and was able to get the case number from the Dallas County Courthouse to continue the lawsuit.

Shortly after, I received a letter from Mr. Greco, dated August 13,1993, telling me the court date was scheduled for November 22, 1993. I was very pleased and excited I finally had a court date, and I also had a lawyer who was going to actually do something to assist me in getting what was legally mine from the Royall National Bank.

A couple of weeks after getting the letter about the court date, I received a call from Mr. Greco for me to meet him. When I arrived, he told me he could not work on my case now. He didn't or wouldn't explain why he couldn't work on it any longer. He just gave me back the court documents I had left in his office. He also told me the court date was no longer in process.

Naturally, I left there feeling pretty defeated. All I could think was, REALLY???

Chapter 13

THE "RUN-AROUND" CONTINUES

Even though I felt defeated, I was not going to give up. I realized that I would still need to do whatever it would take, which I was certain was going to involve more research and investigating. Even though I was looking for another attorney, I knew I needed to keep watching for other evidence to prove the illegal action Royall National Bank had taken. And I still could hear Aunt Birdie telling me about her vow to bring her family's truth to light.

One trip I took was to Austin to the public library where I learned that even though Farmers and Citizens Saving Bank started in 1906, the Texas Bank Directory didn't show the bank's existence until 1922. Our bank number had been #75. This was only four years before the bank was stolen from its depositors and stockholders.

I continued to go to the libraries in Houston, Austin, Galveston, and San Antonio to research any information they may have in regards to the Farmers and Citizen's Savings Bank's history. I also went to the Dallas library many times, but their information was very limited. I even went to many museums to investigate Texas' history and to Brenham, Texas, because that was where Texas' original White House had been located. I was willing to travel wherever if I thought I could find the information I so desperately needed.

I also went to the Federal Deposit Insurance Corporation to file a complaint because during the time that Farmers and Citizens Savings Bank was opened, every business had to have insurance. I had received a letter on October 22 ,1996, from a Mrs. Apperson, who informed me that she was forwarding my complaint to the supervisory jurisdiction. I called Mrs. Apperson after I received her letter. She asked me to come to her office, which was in downtown Dallas.

So, I went to her office the next day. After being seated, she came right to the point. She candidly stated, "The matter regarding the Farmers and Citizens Savings Bank in Palestine was an issue where the insurance company did not have enough money to pay."

I looked at her and she stared back at me, offering no other words of explanation. I left there thinking, "Just another dead-end meeting."

On another one of my trips to Palestine, I went by the Anderson County Tax office, and I happened to meet another lady there, Mrs. Logans, who was taking care of some personal business. I asked her if she knew anything about the

Farmers and Citizens Savings Bank. She looked at me as if she had seen a ghost. She asked me and my friend, who drove with me to Palestine, to meet her at her office. She gave me the address and some directions.

After I arrived, she started to explain to me how prejudiced the people in Palestine were. I told her about my research. She invited me to come and stay with her for a few days. She really wanted to try and help me. We became friends, and I took her up on her offer. After a few times of visiting with her, she told me about the oil well that was on her grandmother's property. The Railroad Commission had told her that if the well had been listed in her grandmother's name, they couldn't change it.

Mrs. Logan took me to the farm that was on her grandmother, Mrs. Morrow's property. I was surprised to see that there was a large oil well there … AND… it was still pumping oil after all of these years.

We drove back to her house and sat down in the kitchen. She fixed us some tea, and then began to tell me about the deposition she had found. It had been signed by a notary so it could be used against her grandmother. She brought the papers to the kitchen and showed me the "family names" of those who were supposedly entitled to receive the money from the oil wells that were still on her grandmother's property.
Mrs. Logans went on to explain how there were two to

three white men who would come to the Negros homes to do business on Sunday afternoons. They wanted them to sign the paper to list their land for drilling purposes. They would tell the owners that they would deposit $1 into their account for the first 6 months and then they would renew it. She went on to say, no one ever even received the $1. They were lied to from the very beginning.

When these men came to Mrs. Morrow's daughter's house, they came with the goal of getting her to sign the papers. They sent her husband around to the side of the house while they took her signature. Then when these men got back to the office, they would put blank sticky papers on the signed paper. It was at their office that they would then sign Mr. Morrow's and Elizabeth's name, making a mark for them to supposedly represent their signature.

Mrs. Logans was surprised to see her grandmother's name on the inventory list of the Farmers and Citizens Savings Bank with a circle around the number next to her name. After reading the deposition, she learned that Mr. Walker, who was the one notarizing this paperwork, had worked directly for Royall National Bank for 13 years. He had actually been the one to notarize her grandmother's and family's documents—but his notary authorization had expired.

The oil well on Mrs. Morrow's property was still operating with an electronic pump, and it had a sign at the entrance coming on to her property that read, "Private Property." Mrs. Logans and her family members wondered who the royalties from that oil well were going to that was on her grandmother's property.

While continuing my search for someone to help me, I was told to get Mr. Jones' help. He lived in Kansas, so my friend, Mrs. Bennett, and I flew to Kansas City to meet him. After showing him the court documents that I had received about the Farmers and Citizens Savings Bank, he was both shocked and surprised that they could get away with doing such an unfair and unjust act like the one they had done.

He left the room for a short moment, and when he returned, he told me he had called a friend of his to see if he could come over to also take a look at these court documents. He had known his friend, Mr. Everman, for years because they had gone to school together. When Mr. Everman arrived, Mr. Jones showed him the documents. Mr. Everman was truly surprised, as well, and said, "I'm sorry to say I've heard of things like this happening, but I've never seen such a mess."

Mr. Everman continued to say, "My sister, Mrs. Booker, works for the Federal Reserve. She may be able to help you." He said, "I will send her a copy of your Aunt Birdie's stock certificate, which shows she had 88 shares of stock in the Farmers and Citizens Savings Bank."

I also explained to him that I was the one who owned the stocks now, and I lived in Texas. I had been offered $300,000.00 for the stocks approximately 20 years earlier. I now believe the stock is in the name of Capital One and Compass Bank.

I went on to explain that I was told that the stock certificate that was originally owned by Birdie, was now registered in the name of Mrs. Gunn. I need to know from you, if possible, whether the stock certificate from the New York Stock Exchange, which has Sarah Gunn's name on it, is in fact still viable and translates into stock ownership in Capital One? I'm asking because the Federal Reserve still has it under my name.

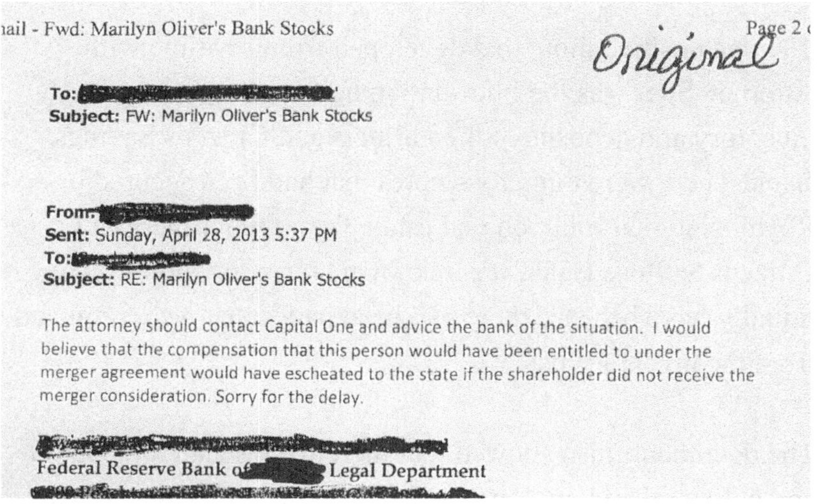
ail - Fwd: Marilyn Oliver's Bank Stocks Page 2

Original

To:
Subject: FW: Marilyn Oliver's Bank Stocks

From:
Sent: Sunday, April 28, 2013 5:37 PM
To:
Subject: RE: Marilyn Oliver's Bank Stocks

The attorney should contact Capital One and advice the bank of the situation. I would believe that the compensation that this person would have been entitled to under the merger agreement would have escheated to the state if the shareholder did not receive the merger consideration. Sorry for the delay.

Federal Reserve Bank of Legal Department

Mrs. Booker's response was that my stock was still good in both Capital One and Compass Bank, who merged with Royall National Bank in 1996, and Compass later changed its name to BBVA in 2019, and then merged with PNC in 2021. The stockholders should have been notified when Farmers and Citizen's Savings Bank was taken over on May 3, 1926, and was then merged into Royall National Bank on May 10, 1926. Mr. Griggs signed the merger, but instead of being notified, they illegally sold the 243 pieces of stock. Since the stockholders weren't notified, the money should still be in Texas, but that's part of the problem—the money is nowhere to be found.

She closed the conversation by suggesting that Mrs. Oliver should hire an attorney.

The one positive thing that developed from my time with Attorney Shor was the information he found regarding the inventory and deposits of the Farmers and Citizens Savings Bank. There were numerous notes that had been secured by Royall National Bank on real estate from the Farmers and Citizens Savings Bank. It's unknown how many notes there initially were because there had been pages that were removed from the inventory list.

The documents also showed that there were secured pledges and collateral and unsecured notes that were also placed with the Royall National Bank. But within these notes there were several stock certificates that were listed with the inventory of the Farmers and Citizens Savings Bank. There was also in the listing that Arkansas Baptist College had $885.60 deposited into the Farmers and Citizens Savings Bank that was given to the Attorney Davis for services toward lawsuits. There were other deposits that were given to him for services rendered for lawsuits.

They also showed the face value of notes were $74,984.80, Real Estate value was $22,998.99, furniture and fixture value was $1,657.52, and cash collected prior to the time of inventory was $3,132.78—all of which totaled $102,773.09.

In 2010, I sought the wisdom of some financial advisors. I went to Nexus Financial Company and met a woman, Miss Eastland. After sharing the details of my case, she tried to find out if the Farmers and Citizens Savings Bank had invested in anything.

315

January 28, 2010

Marilyn Gardner
4021 W. Northgate Dr. #222
Irving, TX 75062

Marilyn,

We have not been able to determine a value on your stock certificates through BNY Mellon. Holly has suggested that we open an account, deposit the certificates and allow our broker/dealer to change the registration to your name and attain a value for you.

Attached you will find all the necessary forms to open the account and deposit the certificates. The original stock certificates will be needed from you along with the applications.

I have highlighted the areas to be completed and flagged the necessary areas for you to sign. Once you have signed, return to our office in the enclosed envelope.

If you have any questions, or need help, feel free to call me.

Regards,

Susan Eastland
Assistant to Holly Carroccio
Nexus Advisors, L.L.C.
10000 N. Central Expy, Suite 1200
Dallas, Texas 75231
seastland@finsvcs.com
972-348-6307

When she contacted the New York Stock Exchange, she managed to get the name of the Bank of Balboa, Compass Bank, and Capital One, but they refused to give her any more information. Miss Eastland looked at me and commented, "Do they have any idea who we are?"

This was a part of their business. They were supposed to give them that information. Miss Eastland had her assistant, Miss Carroccio, call me and come into the office so I could open an account and allow their broker/dealer to change the registration to my name for BNY Mellon "Bank of New York" to make deposits from the stock certificate under Birdie Gardner, which I now owned.

Initially, in May 2010, they opened an account for me and deposited $5.00 into it. In June, they deposited another $5.00 into this same account.

On May 10, 2010, I received a letter from The National Financial Service saying they couldn't identify the certificate because of the handwriting on the certificate. Miss Carroccio informed me that they had to send my stock to the MML Investor Services, LLC, under someone else's name, and they were going to be sending my stock certificate back to me.

National Financial Services LLC

	Security deposited is a non-transferable issue. Company currently does not support or employs an outside agent to support re-registrations.		Certificate(s) presented are photocopies. -NFS DOES NOT HOLD COPIES
	Security deposited has been deemed worthless. ☐ **"No Stockholders Equity"** ☐ **"Adjudicated Bankruptcy"**		Statements and/or Receipts of assets held away cannot be deposited into your brokerage account.
	Security deposited requires the attached form to be completed.		COD certificate(s) cannot be supported in your brokerage account.
	Security presented is not certificated.		Bond(s) presented are compounded interest.
	Security presented is a promissory note.		Bearer issues requires proof of ownership be attached with the deposit.
	Security presented is a privately held issue. Information regarding the security cannot be ascertained.		Certificate(s) deposited are non-negotiable registered in another nominee name or custodian name.
	Certificate presented is not on file with the current transfer agent.		Erroneous registration or custodian.
	Certificate (s) have been escheated to the state.		Transfer agent will not support re-registration without converting the asset to the underlying security.
	Certificate (s) have been reported lost and subsequently replaced.		Security presented is a US Savings bond.
	Company/Issuer dissolved. -Company has been liquidated.		Security presented for deposit is a Limited Partnership, which can not be supported in your brokerage account.
	Shares were sold through an odd-lot buy back.		Security presented is a Mutual Fund, which can not be supported in your brokerage account.
	Certificate(s) are mutilated.		Expired rights/warrants/note/bonds.
	Transferability of the enclosed requires a substantial fee. $______	X	After careful review we were able to identify that the certificate is hand written, dated in and no valid agent has been located. Since we are unable to confirm the validity of this certificate, it is being returned to the client's address of record.
	Missing past payable or future payable coupons.		

ACCOUNT	CUSIP	DATE
JAV-297380	307990341	05/26/10

QUANTITY	DESCRIPTION
88	FARMERS & CITIZENS SAVINGS BANK

When I received the stock certificate, the name it was issued under now was a Mr. Perry from Fidelity Brokers Service,

LLC. It also said that this stock was worth 201 shares with the Panera Bread Company.

20100312336825

Fidelity INVESTMENTS
F007 [illegible]

Fidelity Brokerage Services, LLC
10 Memorial Boulevard
Suite 102
Providence, RI 02903

depositing for custody

Date: 03/12/10

We received the following securities:

Name (account owner): Mark A Perry

Account Number / Type: 236-111953

Delivered by (if different from account owner):

Quantity (shares)	CUSIP	Description (security name)	Certificate Number
34	69840W108	Panera Bread Co	PA 9942
30	69840W108	Panera Bread Co	PA 10588
39	69840W108	Panera Bread Co	PA 11208
31	69840W108	Panera Bread Co	PA 11924
40	69840W108	Panera Bread Co	PA 12603
27	69840W108	Panera Bread Co	PA 13301

Received By: Tim Dunn
(Branch Representative Name)

Signature: [signature]

THIS RECEIPT DOES NOT CONSTITUTE A SALE
Fidelity Brokerage Services LLC Member NYSE, SIPC

382748.3.0

I find this to be very strange that they have to submit the stock under someone else's name and even stranger that they said they couldn't identify the certificate because of the handwriting on the top. They also said that since they are unable to confirm the validity of this stock certificate, it is being returned to the client's address that is on record. Since the stock certificate was submitted under Mr. Perry's name, why did they send it back to me? Because up until now, they had been refusing to acknowledge the stock certificate had any value to me at all. My next question is, "What happened to Sarah Gunn?"

In March of 2020, I decided to go to Capital Bank in Arlington, Texas. I spoke to Mr. Warren, and I informed him that I had a stock certificate that was purchased in the Farmers and Citizens Savings Bank in Palestine, Texas. He advised me that he would be able to assist me in opening an account for the stock certificate. He confirmed that the bank had merged with Compass Bank in Palestine, Texas. He asked me if I had a copy of the certificate with me. I didn't have it with me. He told me to meet him at his office in Fort Worth, Texas, the next day.

When I arrived at the bank the next day, he had a lady try to open an account in my name and to change the stock certificate over to me. When she went into the computer and started inputting the information to open the account, a strange look came over her face. She called him over so he could see what was coming up on the computer. They had the bank manager come over to try and find out what was wrong with the information. The manager seemed to be very curious about the stock certificate because it was so old—they didn't print stock shares anymore. Now, they have a Cusip. She was also surprised that the stock had originated from the Farmers and Citizens Savings Bank from Palestine, Texas.

Mr. Warren then told me that I needed to come back the next day, so they could further investigate what was wrong with the information on the certificate. When I arrived at the bank the first time to open the account, Mr. Warren was so eager to assist me. When I arrived the next day and walked into the bank, he couldn't even look me in the face. He dropped his head and looked down at the floor, as if I wasn't there.

So, I went to the cashier's window and explained to them that I was looking for someone who could assist me in opening an account with the bank, in order to deposit Aunt Birdie's stock certificate. They then told me that I would have to contact the corporate office because they would be the one handling the situation. When I tried to call the corporate office, which was located in Birmingham, Alabama, they said they couldn't help me because the computers were down.

I realize things were getting difficult because Covid was already trying to destroy the world. However, the circumstances here were lining up as usual. I didn't understand why it was so hard for them to try and act so innocent … like I wasn't aware of the fact that the stock was now in another person's name.

Chapter 14

WILL THIS EVER END?

Needless to say, after 40 years, one can become more than tired and willing to give up. However, for some reason, that is not my plan.

Dr. Williamson, Jr.

One of the Farmers and Citizens Saving Bank's shareholders was Dr. St. John Williamson, Jr. He was a descendent of Anderson County. Dr. Williamson has maintained the legacy of his family, keeping his heritage alive. Dr. Williamson was the son of the attorney, St. John and Mary Elizabeth Jones Williamson. He attended elementary school in Palestine and did his high school work at Lincoln in Palestine and at Bishop College in Tyler, Texas. After completing his Junior College work at Butler, he entered Hampton Institute in Virginia where he received his B.S. degree. In 1942, he received his M.A. degree from the University of Iowa, and a Ph.D from the same institution in 1948. His father, attorney St. John Williamson, Sr., was the lawyer for the Farmers and Citizens Savings Bank in Palestine, Texas.

Mr. Williamson, Sr's relative, Wallace Jefferson, had also become an attorney, who later held a position on the Texas Supreme Court. When I heard about him, I felt like it would be a good connection because of his family association with another stockholder from Farmers and Citizens Savings Bank.

So, I emailed Justice Jefferson to let him know that I had been doing research on the Farmers and Citizens Savings Bank merger. I informed him that I had documents and a picture of the bank officers that had been taken in 1917. I also had documents showing where Mr. Grigsby, the CEO of Royall National Bank, had gone to the judge's chambers in the district courts and petitioned the court for Farmers and Citizens Savings Bank to be put into receivership under his supervision at the Royall National Bank.

I also went to the Historical Museum and the Houston Public Library for more information, where I found a copy of where Mr. Williamson had entered a plea of intervention for his land. Your family tree, tracing back to your direct descendants were the officers of the bank. Your father, Mr. Jefferson, was the son of Mrs. Johnnie Mae Williamson, who left Palestine in the 1920's—perhaps after this injustice.

After Mr. Jefferson received the email. He had his secretary call me to see when I would be able to come to Austin, so he could see all the documents that I had mentioned in the email. After we set a date, my friend and I drove to Austin, Texas. We were excited about meeting Mr. Jefferson. When he entered the room my friend started setting up the slide, so I would be able to explain each court document to him.

Mr. Jefferson was surprised to see the documents that I had showing Mr. Grigsby saying that it would be unjust if they let them continue to operate the Farmers and Citizens Savings Bank in the manner of how they were running it.

He commented, “Now I realize why my family just packed up their things and left Palestine, Texas.” After the meeting, he said he would help me find a lawyer who would take my case. He knew a lot of lawyers, but he also knew that finding the right one who would do the right thing may be a little hard to find, but he was going to see what he could do to help me.

In April 2020, I received a call from a Mr. Graves, who stated that Mr. Jefferson had given him my number, and had recommended him to take my case. He told me that he was in the Dallas area, and he wanted to meet with me before he left town. I called Mr. Jefferson to confirm that he had given Mr. Graves my telephone number. Mr. Jefferson’s secretary told me that he had recommended him. I then called Mr. Graves back and I told him I would meet him the next day.

He told me to choose the location which I did, and I called him back. He told me to bring all of the information that I had shown Mr. Jefferson and he also wanted to get copies of the court documents that I had. I didn’t feel comfortable just letting him have the copies of all of my research. He tried to reassure me that he was going to do everything to get all of the depositors and stockholders their money back.

Mr. Graves also told me that he had done some research on it and that Chase Bank and Wells Fargo Bank were responsible for holding up our money. He said that everyone in his office was going to get a copy of it, and go over it to make sure they wouldn't miss anything.

Mr. Graves also told me to stop writing the book. I was going to need the information that he was going to give me for the ending. I should have known something was wrong with this law firm. But I tried to believe that Mr. Jefferson wouldn't recommend a lawyer to me that would turn out to be so crooked.

After a couple of weeks, Mr. Graves had assigned Mr. Matthew to handle my case. I explained to him how I had gotten the court documents. He told me he was going to Palestine, Texas, to do some research. I told him it was going to be hard because they tried to cover up the injustice that had been done. He told me that he would be calling me back when he returned from the trip to Palestine.

After the day came and passed when he was supposed to have gone to Palestine and I didn't receive a call from him, I called him. He said he couldn't find anything. I then asked him about

Sarah Gunn. He said that he found that she was a little old lady who lived there, but she didn't have anything.

His lack of support and providing any legal information went on for two years. He kept putting me off, and he was always on his way to Palestine or was just coming back, but it never made any difference because the results were always the same—he couldn't find anything.

I eventually got tired of hearing all of his lies. I knew it was time to get rid of him and that law firm. I also realized that all they had wanted was my research to see what I had previously found out. When I told them about Mrs. Morrow's case where they were tricking them into signing oil leases for $1 on Sunday afternoons and then going back to the office and putting some paper over the signatures and changing it, Mr. Matthew told me he needed more information like that.

I knew he was lying to me. He wasn't going to continue to make trips to Palestine to do more research. I'm not sure he ever took a trip to Palestine. Everything they did and said was a complete lie.

I kept them for as long as I did because of Mr. Jefferson, but now I'm not so sure if they all didn't get paid off, like some of the others who suddenly quit helping me.

This is when I knew I had to get rid of them.

So, after 4 decades of the same run-around, I knew the only answer was not to seek another attorney. All of their efforts combined were basically useless.

However, I did decide to take the advice of Miss Jackson and write this book. I wish I could tell you that everything has been settled at this point, but unfortunately that is not the case.

I guess what I can say is, “Stay tuned for Volume 2.” (I hope I’m kidding!)

THE FAMILY LEGACY

MR. GREEN GARDNER

Green Gardner
May 5, 1847 - October 20, 1927

Green Gardner was the man who built generations. Green Gardner's life emphasizes one of resilience, determination, and leadership during one of the most challenging eras in American history. On May 5, 1847, while a slave, he worked on the Elias Oldham Plantation in Texas. Green's early years were marked as relentless labor and systematic oppression. Despite these hardships, he immersed as a symbol of progress, leaving a lasting legacy for his family and community.

Green was the eldest of eight children, born to Henry and Fannie Gardner. He was named Green because of his green eye color. His parents had been relocated to Texas by force. The family endured the brutality of slavery, but remained united, drawing strength from their kinship. Greens early years on the Oldham Plantation, and later on C. L. Butler's plantation, shaped his understanding of resilience and adaptability. After the Emancipation in 1865, he chose to remain on the Butler Plantation as a free man, leveraging his knowledge of the land and relationship with the Butlers to secure resources that were otherwise acceptable to freedom.

Through hard work and perseverance, Green acquired this land, understanding its value as a path to stability and generational progress. His entrepreneurial spirit was matched by his dedication to community upliftment.

He collaborated with Reverend Nathan Oggs to establish four key churches—Providence Baptist, Jerusalem Baptist, Bethel Baptist, and A New Hope Baptist, which became the cornerstone of the local African American community. These churches served as spiritual sanctuaries and hubs for education, community organization and economic empowerment.

Green's vision extended beyond his own achievement. He worked to bring down generational barriers, emphasizing the importance of education. Despite social challenges, he ensured that his son, Allison, would learn to read and write, equipping him with the necessary tools to live in a prejudiced society. This commitment to education shows Green's belief in his transformative power and its role in breaking the cycle of oppression.

A devoted family man, Green married four times and had

seven children, instilling in them values of hard work, faith, and perseverance. His children's names are Allison, Henry, Frank, Garfield, Sam, Lilly B, and Clarisee. His dedication to their growth ensured his legacy would endure, influencing further generations.

Green's life journey, from enslaved laborer to landowner and community leader, is proof of the human spirit's ability to overcome adversity. His contribution to faith and community building, particularly through the church he helped establish, left a firm mark. These institutions became symbols of resilience and collective efforts, nursing hope and unity among African American's, dealing with the challenges of post-emancipation life.

Green Gardner passed away in 1927. His burial site is on the land where he worked. It became a sacred symbol of his enduring legacy. His headstone stands as a witness to his life's work and the value he imparted.

At his funeral, the community gathered to honor a man whose faith, leadership, and dedication transformed countless lives.

Green Gardner's story remains an inspiring example of how resilience, vision, and commitment to the community can create a lasting change, even in the face of immense adversity. His legacy continues to shine as a symbol of courage, hope, and progress for generations to come.

ALLISON GARDNER

Allison Gardner was born on March 12, 1889, in Anderson County, Texas, to Green Gardner and Lizzie Smith, who died during his birth. After slavery ended in 1865, Green worked hard to improve life for himself and his son. He secured jobs for them near Palestine, Texas, with the Austin Butler family, making it the start of his aspirations.

Green, Allison's dad, was determined that his son attended school, which was a rarity for Black people at that time. Although education only went up to the 7th grade, Allison learned to read and do basic math.

When Austin Butler died in 1917, Allison took over as steward of the Butler's estate. Since Sarah Butler, Austin's widow, had no interest in the business, she sold it to Allison for $300, which he paid off quickly.

Over time, Allison bought more land, eventually owning about 1,000 acres and a large cotton gin, becoming the only Black man in Anderson County to achieve such success in the early 1920s.

Louisana

He wanted to start a family. In 1893, Allison married a woman from the Jerusalem community near Palestine, Texas. Her name was Louisiana Kelly. Louisiana was the daughter of Prince Kelly and Hester Kelly Burns. She was born on September 27, 1875. They remained married for 31 years until Louisiana died on November 10, 1924. Louisiana is buried in the Jerusalem cemetery.

Allison and Louisiana had one daughter. Her name was Bertha, but everyone called her Birdie. She was born on February 3, 1895.

Allison became very lonely after Louisiana's death and decided to get married again. He married his second wife, Roxy Womack, in 1925. Born on November 8, 1896, she was the daughter of James and Millie Anderson Womack. She died on December 12, 1972.

Roxie and Allison had three children together: Inez, who was born in 1912, Allison, Jr., who was born April 15, 1929, and Joe Willy, who was born in 1931. Allison fathered a total of 23 children—19 of the children were by women other than his two wives, Louisiana and Roxy.

Allison did not do a lot of manual labor. He had sharecroppers who worked for him. He only had to go around to the farm to check on the sharecroppers, and act like a rich white man. He rode horses on his rounds and preferred black stallions.

He was the first Black man to own a car in Palestine. He had so much money that he could just buy whatever he wanted. It was the local custom for Black people to have to wait until Saturday to go into town. However, Allison would make trips into town on any day of the week he so desired.

Clarence Robinson, Sr. was the next richest Black man in Palestine. Clarence and Allison were the two men who did not like each other. The conflict between Allison and Clarence was over who would have the most power. Allison had bought some property that Mr. Robinson wanted, but Allison would not let him have it.

One of Robinson's sons, nicknamed "Felt," shot Allison in the early part of 1924. Allison was riding his horse on his own property. Little did he know that Felt and his brother were hiding in the weeds. As Allison rode by, Felt shot him in the back. Luckily for Allison he was shot with a shotgun, and most of the pellets missed him. The little stallion he was riding on was very quick; he sensed that someone was in the bushes. The horse picked up his gallop, and Allison bent over, which caused most of the gunshot pellets to miss him. Allison survived the attack and later learned that the boy who had done the shooting was Clarence Robinson, Jr.

In revenge, Allison's brother, Henry Gardner, Sr. (nicknamed Rack), made it his mission to look for and kill Felt. He accomplished this on October 11,1924. Allison's brother was briefly in jail for the murder. Rack was always getting into trouble with the law and was constantly in and out of jail. Since Allison had a lot of money, he took the blame for the killing. Allison hired the best lawyer in town, and it didn't take long for both of them to be set free.

Henry, Rack, Gardner died on February 6, 1928, and is buried in Providence cemetery.

Allison became so prominent in the community that he hired a bodyguard. In those days, inmates could be purchased from the prison system. For $100, Allison bought a man with a fearsome reputation to ward off danger. The bodyguard followed Allison everywhere, including his trips to town, visits to sharecroppers' farms, and even church, providing a sense of security.

Clarence Robinson, seeking revenge for his son's death, hired lawyers from Houston to convict Allison. Robinson spent so much money on legal fees and frequent trips between Houston and Palestine that he eventually had to sell most of his property.

The animosity between Allison and Robinson also led to deceitful dealings. After Allison purchased land that a white man wanted, the men attempted to trade or buy it from him. However, Allison refused to give up the land. Allison fell ill, and rumors spread that this white man had paid a doctor to poison him with arsenic. The doctor allegedly administered small doses over time, misleading Allison about the treatments. Despite the poisoning, Allison endured under the doctor's remarks, "I have given you enough arson to kill two mules. I can't understand why you are not dead yet."

This conflict stemmed from Allison's purchasing the land the white men wanted. At just 60 years old, Allison passed away. True to his proud nature, he requested a $500 Tombstone—a significant amount in 1932. Today, at Jerusalem cemetery, his tombstone remains the largest.

At his death on January 29,1932, Allison had over $10,000 in the bank and owned more than 1,000 acres of land. He had donated property for churches, schools, and a cemetery. His first wife, Louisiana, left her share to their daughter, Birdie.

Allison Bought This Church

BERTHA “BIRDIE” GARDNER

Bertha Gardner was born on February 3, 1895. She was the only child born to Allison and Louisiana Kelly Gardner. She was nicknamed Birdie by her parents. Bertha was Allison Gardner’s first born child. When she was growing up, she was expected to get an education, and her father made her go to elementary school at the age of 6 in 1901. Since in the early 1900’s school only went to the 7th grade, she graduated from the 7th grade in 1908.

Birdie continued her education by enrolling in the Prairie View High School Academy in 1908, and graduated from high school in 1910. After attending Prairie View College for only one year, she earned her teaching certificate in 1911. She got her first teaching job at the age of 16 and began her teaching career at Jerusalem Elementary School in 1911.

She was born with wealth and was never deprived of anything that she wanted. She displayed all of those social grace cards of wealth. She also drove new cars. it was said that she was a Pontiac person. Back in 1947, Birdie had a new blue and white Pontiac. That was her favorite color for cars. Later on, in the 1960’s, she started purchasing Cadillacs.

After she began her teaching career, her father had a house built for her in Palestine, near the water tower on Hamlett Street. She had elegant furniture and décor in her home, including rugs that were so beautiful, no one wanted to walk on them.

When Birdie moved to the city, she would go to all of the social gatherings in town. The country folks from the Jerusalem Community could not attend these events. She had moved into a whole new status category and away from her rule of upbringing. She was invited to all of the big social events in town. These gatherings were hosted by Black doctors, lawyers, teachers, and business owners in Palestine.

Birdie's social groups would plan trips around the country. She joined her friends on train rides to Dallas, Houston, St. Louis, Missouri, Chicago, Illinois, and Los Angeles, California. She had a couple of brothers who lived in Chicago. She would visit them from up to a month at a time and would also visit her sister, who lived in California.

Foster School where Birdie taught

In the early 1920's, she got a job teaching in the city of Palestine. She met Dr. Luther Johnson, who was from Chicago, while visiting her brother one year, and they were married in 1923. Dr. Johnson had a very lucrative medical practice in Chicago. After their marriage, she moved to the city. She had a wonderful life with Dr. Johnson for many years, but the union ended in divorce.

Masters Graduation

Birdie moved back to Palestine and started teaching again. She began dating Dr. Robert E. Holland. He came to Palestine around 1935. He wanted to rent some of Birdie's land for a dairy farm, which they ended up running together. Her dairy farm was located on Anderson County Road 409, near the present day Foster Cemetery.

Dr. Holland opened his medical practice in Palestine at McKnight Plaza. He was supported in his early career by Dr. W. Roberts and Dr. J. H. Dodd. He moved his practice to the Colley Building in downtown Palestine in the mid 1940's and later moved his office to his own building in the early 1950's. His office was located at the corner of Lacey and Fort Street.

They had a wonderful relationship with lots of love and happiness. After several years of just dating, Birdie realized that there was not going to be a future with Dr. Holland. There had never been any talk of marriage in their future, so she ended the relationship. Later, in 1942, Dr. Holland married Aurora B. Smith.

After Birdie and Dr. Holland broke up, Birdie began to see this gentleman, Otis Jolly. She dated him and fell deeply in love with him. They got married in 1943. They were happily married for several years, but then this marriage also ended in divorce.

After her marriage to Otis Jolly failed, she moved to Dallas, Texas, in 1953. Birdie also taught at Providence Elementary School from 1943 to 1948. She later became the principal at Foster Elementary School from 1948 to 1953.

Birdie never had any children, but she always had what she wanted. As a Black person, she was very fortunate. There were very few Black people, especially women, who could live her lifestyle.

Birdie L. Gardner died on December 13, 1984, in Dallas, Texas. She was 89 years old.

She is buried in Jerusalem Cemetery.

AUNT BIRDIE'S INHERITANCE—BILLY, HER NEPHEW

Billy and I became caretakers for Aunt Birdie when she became ill in 1984. Aunt Birdie asked Billy and me to not sell her land; she had over 250 acres of land. It had been in the family for over 100 years. She told us that if we had to sell the land to at least reserve the mineral rights. She also told us not to let her cousin, who lived two doors away from her, have her mother's land. The cousin had wanted the land so badly that she had told lies to her.

When Birdie passed away, the will was in Probate. After the Probate was over in 90 days, Billy tried to sell the land to a Mr. Butler. They had made an appointment to go and talk to attorney Luther Johnson in Palestine, Texas. However, because I (Marilyn) refused to sign the bill of sale, Mr. Johnson advised Mr. Butler to not buy the land. Birdie had asked us not to sell the land because it had been in the family for over 100 years. That is why I couldn't sign to sell it.

Billy and I then left Mr. Johnson's office and came back to Dallas. Mr. Johnson also explained to Billy and me that after we had to move in with Birdie as caretakers in her last days, that the estate wasn't just his. I was entitled to have the property as well because it became community property.

I wasn't aware of what Billy and Mr. Butler were still trying to do. I found out later that Billy had actually sold Mr. Butler some land that Birdie had left in his care, even though the instructions were to not sell it unless he absolutely had to.

Billy didn't have to sell the land. I paid all the bills Aunt Birdie had left behind. Birdie also had $2,000 left in her account to pay her house off. All of her legal fees were paid for by me. She had filed a lawsuit, and I looked for lawyers to take her case that was pending that we had to see to the end.

After I learned about the land being sold, I went to Palestine to pull the documents. I learned that Mr. Butler had insurance on the property with Lawyers Title Insurance Corporation in Dallas, Texas. I contacted Lawyers Title Insurance corporation to inform them that I wanted the land back. It had been sold illegally without my signature, and according to Birdie's wishes, there was no reason for the land to be sold. I was told that I couldn't do that.

I have tried to find a lawyer that would take my case to claim what was legally mine. The other cousin that Billy gave away land to I also did not agree to. Everything that I fought for to be corrected, he would go back and destroy when we were together. Billy later admitted to me that they knew they had frauded me out of my part of the land.

I talked to so many different lawyers about trying to get someone to draw up a transfer form, so I could get Billy to sign it. This was the only way I could legally transfer the stock certificate of the Farmer and Citizens Savings Bank into my name.

I went to a National Association of Royalty Owners (N.A.R.O.) meeting, in San Antonio, Texas. While I was at the meeting, I met the late Mr. Milberger. I explained to him what I was trying to do. He asked me to send him a copy of the stock certificate. He told me that he would get someone to draw me up a transfer of title in the Farmers and Citizens Savings Bank that belonged to Aunt Birdie.

Truthfully, I was surprised because at this point I had not been able to get any lawyer to help me with this stock transfer.

Transferring this stock into my name is what officially gave me the legal right to continue Aunt Birdies' request. Because of Mr. Milberger's faithful efforts and the final stock transfer is the reason I dedicated this book to him.

I thanked him for helping me with the form so I would be able to own the stock certificate now that Birdie was gone. No other lawyers would assist me in getting the form for Billy to sign.

Transfer of Stock Ownership

KNOW ALL MEN BY THESE PRESENTS, that Billy Joe Gardner, [Executrix/Executor] of the Estate of Birdie L. Gardner, Deceased, the undersigned, hereby sells, assigns and transfers to Marilyn Lavonne Gardner for value received eighty eight (88) shares of stock standing in the name of Farmers and Citizens Savings Bank on the books of said institution as per the following certificate, No.121 dated 11 May 1920 for eighty eight (88) shares; and hereby irrevocably transfers all rights of ownership to said stock with full power and hereby ratifying and confirming all that shall be lawfully done under authorization herein granted.

SIGNED, SEALED AND GIVEN AT January, this 8th day of 2003.

HOLLY JAMES
MY COMMISSION EXPIRES
October 18, 2005

Holly James

SIGNATURE GUARANTEED: ESTATE OF Birdie L Gardner, DECEASED

By: Billy Joe Gardner
, [Executrix/Executor]

BIOS

H. L. PRICE

Henry Lee (H.L.) Price, Sr. was born on April 24, 1866, in Anderson County, Texas.

He was the son of Sam and Mary Foster Price. H.L.'s father was born as a slave in Mississippi and migrated to Texas in the 1850's with his slave owner. His mother was the daughter of a white plantation owner. Her family was wealthy and they protected Sam and Mary from any difficult obstacles that could have occurred because of the two different races.

Sam Price, H.L.'s dad, was born in 1833, and Mary, his mother, was born in 1838. Sam was a civic and church leader in Palestine. On July 3, 1885, Antioch Baptist Church purchased the property at 913 East Murchison, and his name was placed on the first Cornerstone of the church.

Henry Lee was known as H.L. to all his friends and business associates. He was a pioneer African American politician and an ardent civic leader. He was a member of the National Association of the Advancement of Colored People (NAACP) and was a devoted worker at the Statewide level. He played a leadership role in many NAACP events, including the voting rights meetings in Houston, Dallas, and San Antonio. He was also a close friend of W. E. King, who was the founder of the Dallas Express Newspaper.

H. L. was a friend of Norris Wright Cuney, who was born on May 12, 1846. Cuney was one of Texas' foremost African Americans from the late 1870's through the 1890's. In 1875, Cuney was elected the first Grand Worshipful Master of the Prince Hall Mason in Texas. He was also a member of the Knights of Pythias and the Odd Fellows. Cuney served as the Customs Inspector/Collector for the Port of Galveston, Texas, from 1872 to1889.

Cuney was one of the leading politicians during the heyday of the Black and Tan segment of the Republican Party. The Black and Tan faction was comprised of both Black and white liberal-minded members, while the smallest segment of the party was called *The Lily White*. Cuney served as the secretary of the Republican Party State Executive Committee from 1886 to 1898 and was the Texas Representative to the National Committee of the Republican party from 1884 to 1896; the Black and Tan control of the Texas Republican party from

1886 through 1900.

After Cuney's death on March 3, 1898, the Lily White gained control of the party from 1900 to 1912. The Black and Tans regained control from 1912 to 1920. H.L. Price attended many state and National Republican party conventions with Cuney. He was also a 33rd-Degree Mason.

H. L. was a friend of William "Gooseneck Bill" McDonald. After Cuney's death in 1898, McDonald assumed the leadership role of the Black and Tans. He continued to lead the faction until 1920. In 1914, McDonald founded an African American Bank in Fort Worth, Texas, called The Fraternal Bank and Trust. This Bank served as a main depository for the state's Black Masonic Lodges.

H. L. Price continued to attend many state and National Republican party conventions with McDonald.

H. L. was the founder and Vice Chairman of the Board of Directors of Farmers and Citizens Savings Bank in Palestine, Texas. It was an African American bank that opened in 1906 and lasted for 20 years 1906 to 1926. He also served as the head cashier of the bank.

H. L. was a real estate developer, as well. The African American city, called Andy, was founded in 1865, after the emancipation of slaves. It was named after Andrew Brad, the largest Black landowner in the area, and was located 10 miles Northeast of Jacksonville and Cherokee county. In 1914, H.L. and several other investors planted the town and formed a development company.

H. L. renamed the community Cuney, Texas, in honor of his son, Wright Cuney Price, who was named after Norris Wright Cuney. The community of Cuney opened a post office in 1917. By 1929, Cuney had two general stores, a blacksmith shop, a cotton gin, a drugstore hotel and school. There were three churches, and the population was 100 people.

On Sunday, August 20, 1944, H. L. Price attended a Revival at Rock Hill Baptist Church in Cuney, Texas. J. A. Gilliam, a white state organizer from the NAACP, had been asked to speak, but was told not to bring other white's with him. H.L. told Rev. Brown, "There's no way that white man is coming by himself to a Black church." And H.L. was right. So when J.A. arrived, Rev. Brown refused to let him speak to the congregation. Then, Rev. Brown and H. L. Price argued over the issue, and the pastor called the police. When the Deputy Sheriff, G.O. Martin, arrived, he shot and killed H.L. Price.

Henry Lee (H. L). Price's position in Texas history is one of great distinction. He made significant contributions to the financial and business world of East Texas. He died on August 20, 1944, and was buried in Price Cemetery near Palestine.

REV. CELLAS B. (C. B.) BROWN

Rev. Cellas B. Brown was born in Marshall, Texas. He was one of four children born to Billy and Mary Hansel Brown. He gave his life to Christ at an early age and to the ministry.

He attended numerous colleges. He met and married Ruby M. Bishop. There were no children born to this union.

Rev. Brown pastored 28 churches in his lifetime. Rev. Brown was the pastor at Rock Hill Baptist Church in Cuney, Texas, when Henry L. Price got into a heated argument because Rev. Brown refused to let an NAACP organizer speak at the revival.

Rev. Brown was truly a church builder. He was also a good carpenter. He cut trees, had the lumber milled, and then had the finished wood brought to the church site.

Rev. Brown was an active supporter of the East Texas Baptist Congress of Christian education. Rev. Brown departed this life on August 4, 1967. He was buried in Lincoln Memorial Cemetery in Dallas, Texas.

E.M. GRIGGS

Rev. Griggs resided in Palestine, Texas, and worked with the orphanage in Austin, Texas. Rev. Griggs earned a B. T. H. degree from Bishop College, Marshall, Texas. In the late 1890's, he served the West Union Baptist Church as their pastor. He was the President of the Farmers and Citizens Savings Bank in Palestine, Texas. His wife, Ethel, received her B.S. degree at Bishop College in 1918-1922 in Marshall, Texas. Ethel Griggs went to several colleges. She served as head of the Home Economics Department at Florida A&M University from 1930 to 1940, and as a Public Health Nutritionist in Louisiana from 1952 to 1964.

E. M. Griggs, while serving as the President of Farmers and Citizens Savings Bank at the time of the merger on May 3, 1926, with Royall National Bank, actually signed the merger on May 10, 1926.

Ethel

CAESAR AUGUSTUS DIAL

Caesar Augustus Dial was born in 1861 and died in 1939. He was the fourth child born to Mr. and Mrs. George Merriam Dial of Palestine, Texas. Mr. Dial, or Professor, as he was often called, graduated from Prairie View State College in 1886 and held a permanent teacher's certificate.

His teaching career extended 53 years. Mr. Dial was a farmer and raised everything his family needed. He was a businessman and part owner in the Johnson, Dial, Jackson cotton gin, which was a hand and steam gin, that could quickly separate the seeds from the cotton.

He was a banker and served as an assistant cashier, as well as the President for the Farmers and Citizens Savings Bank in Palestine, Texas. He was in real estate with Messers, E. A. Swanson, H.L Price, and J. L. Randolph. He was married to Miss Estella Mariam Pryor on January 8, 1901, and there were 10 children to the union. The children are Myrtle, James, Caesar, George, Willard, Julia, Juanita, Zula, Estella, and Vera Dial.

Estella

ABOUT THE AUTHOR

I was born in Texas, moved to New Mexico, later moved to Denver, and then to California. A little later, God sent me back to Texas. It was this move that would put me on the path for my greatest life's mission. Returning to Texas was not my choice, and I wasn't even a little excited about it.

I didn't really understand why God would have me return to a place I left. However, after a couple of years of being back in Texas, I met and married Mr. Gardner. Mr. Gardner was actually the reason God had me return to Texas. It turns out he was a key part of the plan for my life. Unbeknownst to me, Mr. Gardner would be responsible for introducing me to his Aunt Birdie. She is the reason this story is being told.

In an early visit with Aunt Birdie, she informed me that she was rich. However, she said, "If I try to get my money, I will be killed." It was this statement that led me to research the matter. Within six months, Aunt Birdie died. Aunt Birdie's death resulted in my inheritance of her land, mineral rights, and memorabilia. While all of these things were great, they do not compare to the value of the stocks she left me.

The acquisition of the stocks has taken me more than four decades to recover, and I'm still counting. It's arguably one of the most challenging pursuits I have had in my life. I am motivated to push forward because the steps I am taking will help me to right a horrible and illegal wrong that happened to a group of Black bank owners close to century ago—a theft that is literally worth billions of dollars.